T0328454

Cambridge Elements

Elements in Psychology and Culture
edited by
Kenneth D. Keith
University of San Diego

THE PROCESS OF WELLBEING

Conviviality, Care, Creativity

Iza Kavedžija
University of Cambridge

CAMBRIDGE
UNIVERSITY PRESS

CAMBRIDGE
UNIVERSITY PRESS

University Printing House, Cambridge CB2 8BS, United Kingdom

One Liberty Plaza, 20th Floor, New York, NY 10006, USA

477 Williamstown Road, Port Melbourne, VIC 3207, Australia

314–321, 3rd Floor, Plot 3, Splendor Forum, Jasola District Centre,
New Delhi – 110025, India

103 Penang Road, #05–06/07, Visioncrest Commercial, Singapore 238467

Cambridge University Press is part of the University of Cambridge.

It furthers the University's mission by disseminating knowledge in the pursuit of
education, learning, and research at the highest international levels of excellence.

www.cambridge.org
Information on this title: www.cambridge.org/9781108940825
DOI: 10.1017/9781108935616

First published 2021

A catalogue record for this publication is available from the British Library.

ISBN 978-1-108-94082-5 Paperback
ISSN 2515-3986 (online)
ISSN 2515-3943 (print)

The Process of Wellbeing

Conviviality, Care, Creativity

Elements in Psychology and Culture

DOI: 10.1017/9781108935616
First published online: December 2021

Iza Kavedžija
University of Cambridge

Author for correspondence: Iza Kavedžija, ik406@cam.ac.uk

Abstract: *The Process of Wellbeing* develops an anthropological perspective on wellbeing as an intersubjective process, which can be approached through the prism of three complementary conceptual framings: conviviality, care, and creativity. Drawing on ethnographic discussions of these themes in a range of cultural contexts around the world, it shows how anthropological research can help to enlarge and refine understandings of wellbeing through dialogue with different perspectives and understandings of what it means to live well with others and the skills required to do so. Rather than a state or achievement, wellbeing comes into view here as an ongoing process that involves human and nonhuman others. It does not pertain to the individual alone but plays out within the relations of care that constitute people, moving and thriving in circulation through affective environments.

This Element also has a video abstract: www.cambridge.org/wellbeing

Keywords: wellbeing, anthropology, care, conviviality, creativity

ISBNs: 9781108940825 (PB), 9781108935616 (OC)
ISSNs: 2515-3986 (online), 2515-3943 (print)

Contents

1 Introduction

While the social sciences have historically tended to focus on social problems and pathologies, this Element invites us to think about what it means to live well with others. By exploring living well in its own right, making it a focus of study, we are afforded a new and enlarged view of the person or self and of society at large – a view different to that which arises from attention to the pathological. Without doubt, striving for a better understanding of social problems and crises is of the utmost importance, but studying pathologies can only get us so far when it comes to understanding wellbeing, which is not simply an absence of suffering or an inversion of the problematic, challenging, or undesirable. Living well and wellbeing are, of course, closely related, in complex ways, to negative and challenging aspects of experience. In many cultural settings, suffering and wellbeing are not seen as polar opposites but as mutually constitutive and entwined aspects of the human condition. Departing from this insight, this Element is underpinned by two central and related questions: How do people living in different kinds of situations understand wellbeing and how do they strive to live well despite the many challenges they face?

I approach the discussion of wellbeing through the lens of three conceptual framings, which I refer to as conviviality, care, and creativity. I do not wish to imply that these are the "key elements," "ingredients," or components of wellbeing, or the prerequisites for achieving it. I have chosen these concepts, in the first instance, because they – along with some others including hope, vulnerability, resilience, and happiness – have been at the forefront of much productive work in anthropology in recent years. I draw on anthropological contributions to the discussions of conviviality, care, and creativity, which are not, for the most part, directed at the discussion of wellbeing as such but lend themselves very well to understanding social qualities of wellbeing and their embeddedness in particular cultural contexts. By exploring their relevance for wellbeing, and by making the connections more explicit, I therefore aim to offer a substantive contribution to cross-disciplinary and interdisciplinary discussions – slightly shifting the way we use these concepts along the way. I do this from a distinctly anthropological perspective, namely one that combines theoretical analysis with nuanced ethnographic descriptions based on long-term engagement with research participants and aims at a "thick description" of their experience. Among other things, anthropology has the capacity to draw on ethnographic findings to show us other ways of organizing thought and practice. By attending carefully to the conceptual framings of others, we can better challenge and refine our own ontological and epistemological assumptions. The perspectives of those we meet in the field – our research participants and interlocutors – can and do often encourage us to reconsider what exists and what we can know.

My own research has been mostly carried out in Japan, with older Japanese and, more recently, with young contemporary artists. In *The Process of Wellbeing*, however, I will draw on a broad range of examples. To those less familiar with an anthropological approach, this might seem surprising: Are so many examples from different parts of the world really necessary? Yes, they are, and they are not merely illustrative, although the textured description is helpful in itself. Most importantly, they provide the raw material that allows us to construct the argument. The method here is primarily inductive. Rather than departing from particular hypotheses, straightforward and clearly articulated, which are then "tested," as it were, the inductive approach aims to build arguments gradually from the ground up. Ethnographic theory, at its best, draws on empirical examples from rich ethnographic descriptions; conceptual framings are developed and refined with reference to these descriptions, and stem from them, but are more abstract than the descriptions themselves. Rather than primarily relying on theoretical tools and concepts developed by Western philosophers, then, my departure points consist of concepts originating in the ethnographic description of diverse cultural practices around the world. By focusing on how people in a variety of different settings attend to conviviality, care, and creativity, we are well placed to reconsider, and expand, our understanding of the nature of wellbeing.

1.1 Culture and Wellbeing

Anthropologists have long concerned themselves with the different ways in which people not only live but reflect upon their own lives and with how they negotiate social models and personal preferences. Countless ethnographies have been written in which we may discern an underlying concern with what a good life is for a particular group of people, and yet, surprisingly, questions of wellbeing and happiness have rarely been explored explicitly. Neil Thin (2008) attributed anthropology's evasion of the topic of happiness to four dominant influences in the social sciences more generally: alongside "anti-hedonism" and "moral relativism," he identified what he described as "clinical pathologism" and "anti-psychologism." The former refers to the prevalent attitude among social scientists that pathologies and problems are somehow more worth studying than the good aspects of life. The latter, meanwhile, has constrained analysis of the emotions either through the social constructionist rejection of the psychologists' universalist assumptions about the unity of human psychological makeup or through a cognitivist resistance to the study of emotional experience (Thin, 2008, pp.138–150).

On the other hand, happiness and its relationship to the good life have long been an overt object of attention among philosophers (cf. Brülde, 2007; Tiberius, 2004) as well as psychologists and social psychologists. The importance of wellbeing and related topics in psychology seems to be growing, and the study of positive experiences is fast becoming one of the central research interests in the field of personality psychology (Suh & Oishi, 2004). The philosopher Valerie Tiberius (2004) distinguished substantive accounts of wellbeing from its formal analysis, stressing that while cultural differences might be relevant for the first, they do not undermine the latter philosophical project, which strives to reveal the nature of wellbeing as a universal notion. As such, the philosophical project mostly limits itself to formal analysis of the concept, leaving the substantive accounts, which point to differences in sources and causes of wellbeing, to other disciplines. To date, this has mostly been undertaken by social psychologists comparing large samples of quantitative data. The need for other types of data, including in-depth ethnographic accounts, has been explicitly recognized by practitioners in the field (Diener & Suh, 2000; Suh & Oishi, 2004). Much has been written on the topic of wellbeing in cross-cultural psychology, but the contributions from anthropologists remain relatively scarce.

1.2 Wellbeing and Happiness

At this point, it is fruitful to examine more carefully some of the various key terms mentioned so far, particularly "wellbeing" and "happiness," and their interconnections. Happiness is often equated with subjective wellbeing (SWB) (cf. Diener & Suh, 2000; Thin, 2008). Psychologists use the notion of SWB as comprising people's affective and cognitive evaluations of their lives (Diener & Fujita, 1995, as cited in Triandis, 2000, p. 14). These evaluations include people's emotional reactions to events, their moods, and judgments they form about their life satisfaction, fulfillment, and satisfaction with domains such as marriage and work. Thus, SWB concerns the study of what laypeople might simply call happiness or satisfaction. Furthermore, "SWB is one measure of the quality of the life of an individual and of societies" (Diener et al., 2003, p. 405). The notion of wellbeing triggers two opposed yet linked reactions among many anthropologists, as Lambek (2008, p. 115) has pointed out: On the one hand, the idea of measuring wellbeing bears resemblance to certain modernist interventionist ideas that have caused a number of difficulties – one need only be reminded of the pitfalls of social modernist planning, for instance. On the other hand, the need for engagement with the political, and the related need for the study of ethics in social action, makes engaging with ideas of wellbeing crucial. In order to make critical statements about aspects of social action, one needs some kind of description or criterion of wellbeing.

The notion of wellbeing has also been a focus of interest in the fields of economics and development studies, typically in the form of something to be measured and quantified through what scholars take to be either its constituents (e.g., freedom) or its determinants (e.g., services or goods that contribute to it) (Dasgupta, 1993). These analyses of wellbeing were often equated with, or paralleled by, discourses about "quality of life." A notable example is the so-called capability approach, according to which capabilities are understood as peoples' freedom to realize various aspects of their wellbeing (e.g., Nussbaum & Sen, 1993; Robeyns & Biskov, 2020). Efforts have been made to encompass various aspects of wellbeing within a holistic notion that extends beyond material goods and economic wealth (Gough & McGregor, 2007). The discourse of wellbeing and quality of life has served as one that unifies claims about health, rights (political and human), freedom, and education (Jiménez, 2008). In this respect, it is not unlike human rights discourse, which has been used both as a powerful tool for empowerment and as a delimiting discourse, defining a certain type of personhood, preferably independent and agentive.

Wendy James (2008) helpfully analyzed the concept of wellbeing alongside the more established concept of welfare. Despite their similar usages in the context of social theory and policy, the meanings of these notions are quite different:

> "Welfare" can only be imagined, and put into practice, in the context of a very clear social whole, where responsibility can be located for the ongoing lives of persons to whom some obligation is publicly acknowledged. . . . On the other hand, "wellbeing" as a concept is not geared to the needy. In contemporary usage, in practice, it is part of a gloss on the promotion of consumer interests in the enhancement of "self." (James, 2008, pp. 69–70)

Wellbeing in this sense moves beyond the mere satisfaction of needs. James drew attention to a difference in the connotations of these terms and the contemporary usage of the rather postmodern term "wellbeing" in the contexts of humanitarian endeavors or by administrative authorities. One of the problems with the use of the term "wellbeing" is that it often obscures an underlying modern or modernist project of welfare (James, 2008). Without any intention to devalue the attempts of social scientists and policy makers to use this kind of concept in order to build holistic, more effective and humane social policies, it is important to note that there is significant ambiguity surrounding the present usage of the concept of wellbeing in terms of the relation between individual self-enhancement and the wider social whole.

What is the relation between wellbeing and happiness? Many of the authors who consider wellbeing defined primarily as subjectively experienced and reported, or SWB, have further equated wellbeing with happiness. Some authors conceive them as basically different expressions of the same notion or at least do not make an explicit distinction (cf. Diener & Suh, 2000; Thin, 2008). On the other hand, and as indicated by cross-cultural contributions of psychologists in the volume by Diener and Suh (2000), happiness seems to be both variously conceived depending on time and place and differently valued in relation to its contribution to wellbeing. In other words, what happiness means for people, and how important it is considered to be for their wellbeing, varies across cultural contexts and perhaps for different individuals. This has been explored by philosophers through the notion of "prudential value" or "final value," which refers to a good as an end in itself. If the good life or wellbeing is formally defined by philosophers in terms of what has a final value for a person, then one should ask what these values are. Is happiness the only final value? It is certainly possible that there are other final values such as meaningful work, social relations, or friendship, among others (Brülde, 2007). From an anthropological viewpoint, focusing on substantive accounts rather than formal definitions, happiness cannot therefore be equated with wellbeing, even though it could represent a central value for some.[1]

1.3 What Is Wellbeing?

In light of these different approaches and perspectives, it is important to outline what wellbeing means in the context of this Element. Although I am sympathetic to some of the criticisms of the concept voiced by anthropologists, I believe that wellbeing remains a useful concept, well worth retaining.[2] One reason for this is quite simply its widespread scholarly use in recent years. While I depart from SWB, for the sake of continuity with the plethora of studies in psychology, economics, and social policy that rely on its large-scale measurement, my aim is to offer an anthropological enlargement and refinement of the term's definition and use.

---

[1] For a discussion of happiness and values in diverse ethnographic contexts, see Kavedžija and Walker (2016).

[2] Some of the objections revolve around the idea that it is not an "experience-near" concept, unlike "happiness," which most people seem to recognize (Thin, 2012). Happiness might indeed offer a greater sense of familiarity: we might all feel we know what we mean by it, yet this might be a problem in itself and a source of confusion.

One helpful approach to wellbeing by anthropologists suggests it is a positive state for communities, groups, and individuals (Mathews & Izquierdo, 2009). Although experienced subjectively by individuals, it is culturally framed, inflected by social contexts and particular sociohistorical circumstances and expectations. And while people in different places might have various ideas about what comprises wellbeing, these ideas and experiences, Mathews and Izquierdo (2009) argued, can be compared. They wrote, "Well-being is an optimal state for an individual, community, society, and the world as a whole" (p. 5). Although the link between these different levels of analysis is important, the definition of wellbeing as an optimal state is not, however, without its problems. First, it seems potentially unattainable and exclusive – it may exclude some people or groups, and even appear as an impossibly high bar for most people, most of the time. Furthermore, focusing on wellbeing as a "state" leads us to think of it in static terms – as something to be achieved – and to lose sight of its processual and relational nature. The strength of this definition is instead in the emphasis both on the individual and on larger collectives such as a community or society. This emphasis on the social qualities of SWB has also been highlighted by some other authors (e.g., Thin, 2012) and is worth insisting upon.

Let us then consider what it might mean to say that wellbeing is in some fundamental ways social. It is not merely to say that sociality is valued or that people need social connections to thrive. It is also to recognize the social forces that structure health and suffering, such that some groups of people are distinctly at a disadvantage (Farmer, 2004; Kleinman, Das, & Lock, 1997). This is clear enough when it comes to illness, suffering, or discrimination, but this meta-individual level affects wellbeing, too. In other words, if suffering can feel deeply individual, private, and personal, so too can wellbeing.

I believe it is more helpful to consider wellbeing an intersubjective process, rather than a subjective state. It is not objective or static either, even though the objective circumstances and evaluations of others, concerning the status of one's own wellbeing, do have an appreciable effect. Focusing on care, conviviality, and creativity, as I do here, has the distinct advantage of drawing attention to wellbeing's processual nature as well as its dynamic, intersubjective qualities. By looking at wellbeing through these three theoretical frames we become aware of the effort, mastery, and skill involved in living well together; entanglement with others in relations of care and dependence on others; and the temporal unfolding of wellbeing when looking at creative processes. The latter allows us to focus on the process itself, and on collaborative participation in the moment, rather than on achievement or final products.

For the purposes of this discussion, then, I define wellbeing as the intersubjective process of living and feeling well. Crucially, it does not pertain to an individual alone but plays out within the relations of care that constitute people. It has an important moral and political dimension alongside the affective dimension more directly implied in notions of "feeling good" or "feeling well." Wellbeing is not an achievement or a state; it is not static but an ongoing process that involves individuals, communities, and societies.

1.4 Wellbeing in a World of Want

It might be objected that a focus on wellbeing is a luxury: something one can only begin to entertain once basic needs and living conditions have been satisfied. What constitutes the good life is indeed the kind of question reflected upon by those who have what the ancient Greeks called *scholé*, a spare moment, the leisure to pursue such issues. It has, not unreasonably, been suggested that *scholé* was the source of philosophy. In this light, it might seem plausible to argue that a preoccupation with ideas of wellbeing – along with a direct pursuit of wellbeing in any of its various guises – could be lumped with other so-called post-materialist values. This latter notion is based on the idea that changing dominant values in modern industrialized societies reflect the relative security brought about by technological and economic change, which significantly lowered the likelihood that people would die young due to starvation or disease (Inglehart, 2000). This may well be true, yet I am convinced, as an anthropologist, that some idea of what constitutes the good life pertains in some form to every human society. Striving for a better understanding of the diversity of these ideas, attentive to potential points of convergence and divergence, is crucial. It is also feasible even where the available data were not collected with this aim in mind.

Hardship, scarcity, poverty, and various other consequences of civil war are no strangers to many living in Sierra Leone, including the Kuranko, with whom the anthropologist Michael Jackson (2011) worked on several consecutive field trips.[3] Yet these difficult circumstances have not precluded their thinking about wellbeing. On the contrary, it seems that many of Jackson's interlocutors reflected on their lot in the world with some frequency. What seems to matter is how one bears this lot, and how one goes on living, under the burdens of life – a sentiment encapsulated in the Kuranko saying, "The name of the world is not world. Its name is load" (Jackson, 2011, p. 179). What matters most, for them, is how one copes with life and what it brings, less realizing one's dreams and more

---

[3] Parts of this section have previously been published in an essay in the *Anthropology of This Century*. http://aotcpress.com/articles/singing-empty-belly/.

"a matter of learning how to live within limits . . . . To withstand disappointment and go on in the face of adversity imparts quality to life" (Jackson, 2011, p. 62). According to this view, the needs of others (especially significant others) must be balanced with one's own needs, and wellbeing is to be found within this balance but, as such, always continues to be labile (Jackson, 2011).

The dilemma is made more visible when people struggle to achieve a better, or at least more bearable, life, balancing their obligations to the group (whose support is often precious) with their own aims. This is when the feeling of strain in sharing their scarce resources becomes noticeable, as does the burden of submitting their life course to the plan laid out for them, with the importance of social harmony and custom always in mind. Acute for many Kuranko, this dilemma rings true for most of us, and Jackson indeed attempted to say something about universal human existential issues using the Kuranko example. He did so above all by telling stories, weaving together those stories Kuranko know and retell – those they share or make their own – with the stories of their lives and circumstances. The point stories make is often ambiguous, but that is precisely their strength: rather than simplifying the links between the causes and effects, stories comprise multiple meanings. They have a capacity to teach people how to act in a complex world of changing circumstances and, as Arthur Frank (2010) pointed out, how to make our lives good. Perhaps this is what makes them so well suited for an exploration of wellbeing.

One such story runs as follows:

> There was a man and a woman. They had a child. But the parents died when the child was very young, and the little girl was placed in the care of her mother's co-wife. This woman would prepare rice and sauce and put it on the same platter. All her children would eat from the same plate. But one day the woman divided the food into two portions. One portion was for her own children. The other portion was for her late co-wife's child. And then into this portion the woman put poison. When the child ate this food she began to foam at the mouth, and she soon died. But after she had passed away she sent a dream to her mother's co-wife, saying that she knew about the poison, and how the woman killed her. The stepmother woke up in dismay, saying, "It wasn't me, it wasn't me. You must have eaten that poisoned food elsewhere." The child said, "All right, then; one day you will die and meet me here in lakira, and God will judge whose story is true." After that dream, the child disappeared. She disappeared from this life. (Jackson, 2011, p. 57)

It is hard to know if this means that a punishment will ensue or if the girl disappeared for good with a vain hope. The ending of the story admits of several possibilities and circumscribes an uncertain existence. This story was told to Jackson by an eleven-year-old girl, Sira Marah, who was not an orphan but whose father had left and whose mother was unable to take care of her. The night before she told the anthropologist one of her stories, she came to the spot where he was sitting with a few companions near a fire. Despite her slender physique, her voice was strong and beautiful, more noticeable than that of the two older girls who accompanied her. She had not eaten for two days but her voice was unwavering and her song compelling. It later transpired that Sira had composed the song herself, along with many others, and also had a gift for divination and herbal medicine, and made a living in this way. After her father left, she could no longer afford school fees and stopped her education, so Jackson started wondering if he could help out by paying her fees. In the end, he decided to do so despite having doubts and realizing that Sira had found a way to live, making do with what she had, with her gift. Sira's story illustrates another aspect of wellbeing, central for many Kuranko: endurance and the ability to make do with what one faces in life – singing on an empty belly.

On the other hand, Sira and Jackson's other interlocutors have a strong wish to improve their lot, to have more and make more of their lives. Jackson emphasized the importance of hope, which allows people to envision their lives as more than what they already are, with tomorrow always bringing new possibilities. Young Kuranko, like many other people in this country scarred by war, are often frustrated by an apparent lack of possibilities, for work and for making a life of one's own, and find themselves lacking stability and income, and therefore prospects for starting a family, stuck instead in their present circumstances. Hope is an important element of wellbeing for these young people dealing with the harsh reality of everyday life, facing scarcity and poverty.

Close attention to the Kuranko example brings other questions to the fore: For instance, how does the way people understand themselves in relation to others influence their search for wellbeing? Jackson's work indicates a link between these issues. Some groups of people, like the Kuranko, emphasize the importance of their relationships; in some ways at least they are fundamentally open to others. At the same time, they insist that despite this openness, they cannot really tell what is in others' minds – what their motivations are or how they truly feel. In contrast, people who tend to think that human beings are essentially separate and self-contained (as implied by the term "individual") seem to talk more freely about the emotions and intentions of others. Perhaps those who believe that selves are fundamentally permeable and open tend to be more concerned with demarcating boundaries around the self, while those who consider it to be fundamentally separate emphasize creating bridges with others. How do these opposed ways of thinking about oneself in relation to others mesh with ideas of wellbeing and a striving to live well? The Kuranko example suggests that reconciling the demands set by others with our openness to them is one of the central balancing acts in the ongoing cultivation of wellbeing. In this discussion, in order to make arguments about how wellbeing figures in different cultural settings, we must attend to the different ways in which persons are themselves conceptualized.

1.5 Beyond the Individual

Social scientists and psychologists are increasingly aware that in order to understand what it means to live well, one cannot focus solely on individuals. This is clear in settings such as that described by Jackson but does not only hold true where there is a cultural emphasis on relationships and connections. While the simple dichotomy between individualism and collectivism has been the focus of critique, attending to the emplacement of the individual in the collective and to the social construction of personhood is fundamental for a more inclusive understanding of wellbeing.[4] This is particularly important as many of the dimensions identified in psychological studies do appear to have a very strong social or meta-individual component. Furthermore, Veenhoven (2008) is right to suggest that wellbeing is important for sociology and the social sciences, not merely as an intellectual project but also as one that allows us to improve social systems. Yet, in the same article, he cited work on the limited effects of social inequalities for wellbeing, past a certain income threshold, and pointed to studies suggesting that social welfare regimes do no better than other states at ensuring the wellbeing of their citizens. The problems might be with the specific studies in question, of course, but the implicit contradiction could be attributed to a move between different conceptualizations of wellbeing, hinging on either objective or subjective criteria.

In my view, it is crucial to move beyond the idea of wellbeing as something that pertains to an individual alone. We must also bear in mind that such a discourse has practical and political consequences. If we think of happiness as a matter of individual responsibility and individual choice, we might be empowering some, but we are also failing to highlight the structural nature of some of the problems that befall many others (see also Cabanas & Illouz, 2019). Suffering may be individually experienced, but it is entwined with structural forces operating in society at large, well beyond the individual's own influence – as illustrated by Paul Farmer's well-known work on structural violence (2004). In this sense, studying wellbeing gives us the opportunity to do better social

---

[4] The dichotomy between individualism and collective criticism has come under scrutiny in recent years, along with an increased understanding that such labels cannot account for internal diversity of societies described in these terms, and the use of such dichotomies in therapeutic settings may result in unhelpful stereotyping (Wong, Wang, & Klann, 2018).

science (Derné, 2016). It also allows us to move beyond the discourse of wellbeing as happiness, or to be more precise, happiness as an individual property, and hence individual responsibility.

The problem with conceptualizing wellbeing as subjective is that the descriptor "subjective" can be misleading and problematic. This is not to say that wellbeing is not somehow personal, subjectively experienced, or interior, while at the same time affected by external factors. The problem is that the idea of the subject implied in much academic work, as a self-contained, autonomous individual, often does not correspond well to prevalent understandings of the subject "on the ground," among the people whose wellbeing we are interested in. Of course, simply acknowledging this mismatch does not solve the problem: to conceptualize an expanded subject, or to consider wellbeing as truly intersubjective, is very challenging. My approach here is to develop three complementary concepts, or conceptual frameworks, taken from a range of anthropological research, which I believe are especially useful for arriving at a more nuanced conceptualization of wellbeing as an intersubjective process. These should not be understood simply as components or ingredients of wellbeing, so much as sets of interrelated analytical tools that help to organize our ideas. All three are developed and refined with reference to a range of empirical examples, in many cases drawn from the work of scholars whose aims were quite different from those that concern us here. The first of these, conviviality, refers to endeavors to live well together and the skilled practices that underpin them. The concept highlights how living well with others is not simply a state of affairs, or a one-off achievement, but an ongoing process demanding effort as well as the refinement of the requisite skills. The second, care, which also invites us to attend to the relational and processual nature of wellbeing, brings to the fore people's interdependencies on one another. The third framing, creativity, can be understood as collaborative and improvisational practice and, like the first two, demands that we attend carefully not only to our fellow humans but also to a range of nonhuman companions and others, including the people, the tools, and the materials that surround us. By refocusing our attention to care, creativity, and conviviality, my hope is that a new perspective on wellbeing opens up – one which not only establishes its relational and processual qualities but shows us how wellbeing moves and thrives in circulation through affective environments.

2 Conviviality

We tend to think of wellbeing as a state or achievement of individual people. What might we learn if we instead shift the focus to think of it not as a feature of individual lives and bodies but instead as a thoroughly relational process? I argue in this section that conviviality is a valuable framework for helping us to do this, allowing us to expand and deepen the study of wellbeing along the way. While there is a significant amount of anthropological literature, from a broad range of cultural settings, that addresses ideas of living well together, this work remains largely disconnected from recent scholarly work on wellbeing. One of my aims here, then, is to forge a better link between the two, drawing out the connections while developing conviviality as a potent conceptual framework. By examining a wide range of anthropological sources that rely on detailed ethnographic descriptions of people's experiences of constructing a good life together, we can better see the art and skill involved in living well with others while bringing together considerations of ethics, aesthetics, and politics.

2.1 Living Well Together

Over the past several years, there has been an increasing recognition that wellbeing, while experienced subjectively, should be understood not merely in individual but also in social terms. The community and environment are now routinely listed as significant factors in SWB. Undoubtedly, how we live with others around us affects the way we feel. Some authors have sought to develop a concept of social wellbeing as a way of understanding wellbeing within social structures and larger groups (Baldwin et al., 2020; Keye, 1998). Building on insights from psychology and social epidemiology, Baldwin and her colleagues emphasized that determinants of wellbeing encompass the individuals themselves, those with whom they interact, and their broader social environments. In this work, the authors devised a new framework for measuring neighborhood flourishing, focusing on individuals and their experiences. Yet, scaling up the psychological work on wellbeing is a challenging task, as the work by Baldwin and colleagues attests.

I propose that rather than simply attempting to move the analysis of wellbeing from the individual to the community level (for example, by recognizing the impact that our social and institutional environments have on us as individuals), the social and relational wellbeing might be more fruitfully considered by moving away from the individual as a departure point. As the next section will make clear, humans are always already enmeshed in relations of care with others.

A framework that might help us to consider wellbeing as meta-individual is difficult to capture, however – largely because it is very challenging to discuss the intimate and the institutional realities, organized and informal relationships, that affect wellbeing at the same time. The broader institutional levels might arguably be well captured by measurements such as objective wellbeing indices, including quality of life. Large-scale institutions have long been a focus of much work in sociology and public policy, which highlights the structural effects on individuals. Meanwhile, individual wellbeing and how it plays out on the level of personal or subjective experience tends to be the focus of work in psychology. Policy and advocacy work on happiness and wellbeing tends to focus on either the institutional macro-level or individual health level (Thin, 2012). What requires further attention, therefore, is what bridges the two: work that attends to what happens on the middle ground, between the macro-level (of institutions and nation-states) and the micro-level of the individual. This is what Neil Thin (2012) referred to as the meso-level, encompassing observations of everyday interactions and cultural practices. This is one reason why conviviality is so helpful as a theoretical framework: It effectively foregrounds the acts and practices of living together while attending to the affective dimensions of that experience.

2.2 What is Conviviality?

Living well together is no small feat. Achieving and maintaining harmonious relationships is challenging at times, and considerable effort might be required to navigate social relationships effectively and overcome tensions as and when they arise. Conviviality does not, therefore, simply refer to a blissful state of stability: it encompasses the effort and the skills that are needed in order to live well with others. Anthropologists working in Amazonia have long found that conventional analyses of human societies as relatively stable entities with enduring institutions are simply inadequate for understanding the fluid socialities they encounter in the region. Struggling to understand communal and social life without resorting to sociological explanations or frameworks based around institutions and statuses, Overing and Passes (2000) suggested a more processual approach, involving a move away from the framework of "society" and a focus instead on conviviality, understood as the arts of living together.

"Arts" is a particularly apt expression here, in my view, as it implies a certain level of skill or mastery, while highlighting the aesthetic qualities of living well. Getting along nicely, in other words, living well together, can be seen as something beautiful. Living well together requires crafting, organizing, and maintaining relationships, supporting the right kind of personhood, caring for people in ways that let them thrive and grow, and doing the right thing by others – such aims are ethical as much as political. The arts of living well together present life together as an ongoing process, requiring effort, never static, never quite completed, or definitively achieved. Attending to wellbeing through conviviality requires a focus on process and practice in the interpersonal space. While inherently mundane, it renders this personal process inherently ethical and political.

2.3 Feeling Good Together: Moral Moods and Political Sentiments

> All societies are full of emotions. Liberal democracies are no exception. The story of any day or week in the life of even a relatively stable democracy would include a host of emotions – anger, fear, sympathy, disgust, envy, guilt, grief, many forms of love
>
> (Nussbaum, 2013, pp. 1–2).

Emotions and moods are not simply felt by individuals – they have an important place in the social life of any community, as Nussbaum (2013) pointed out in the opening of her book *Political Emotions*. Recognition that emotions can be political as they underpin and guide social life is widely present in many Amazonian settings. For example, Peter Gow (2000) described the affective backdrop of all social relations among the Piro in terms of *helplessness*, a Piro expression which he argues captures well the existential condition of being alone, of having no social relations to others. To recognize the grief, sorrow, and helplessness of another is permeated with sympathy; in fact, to see another as helpless, in the Piro language, translates more specifically as "to see the grief, sadness, suffering, cuteness or cuddliness of another" (Gow, 2000, p. 47). Babies are a prototype of helplessness – they are born alone, without any social ties, not least because the Piro (like many other Amazonian groups) do not simply assume that the child is necessarily one of their own, a member of their own group, or indeed a fellow human. It must be nurtured and fed appropriate food in order to mature into a human. Until then, it is utterly helpless. This recognition of helplessness leads to a particular emotional disposition that has fundamentally moral underpinnings. Recognizing someone's helplessness invites sympathy and support – people can see them as poor and cute – poor old widow, a cuddly little strange infant, both in need of support. By extending help and providing food, social ties are slowly crafted. In this sense, helplessness for Piro forms an affective precondition for living together and could be thought of as a moral mood and a political emotion. Feelings are not simply private affairs, playing out within the individual person. They have a moral valence and unfold in the context of a community and, as such, can be considered political. Moreover, embodying these dispositions guides moral judgments. We might further describe these dispositions as particular kinds of moral moods (cf. Throop, 2014), as temporally complex and enduring, with a notably visceral, embodied component to them.

Not all feelings that we are socialized to make sense of in the form of emotions are socially generative or supportive of social relations. The most notable and easily recognizable social and political emotion is anger. Of course, the channeling of dissatisfaction and recognition of injustice that anger highlights can lead to resistance and positive social change (cf. Nussbaum, 2013). Left unchecked, however, or deliberately harnessed for dubious goals, it is likely to cause problems. For many Amazonian groups, a display of anger is seen as a clear threat to living well together (Overing & Passes, 2000). Among the Yanomami, infamous (whether rightly or otherwise) for their bellicose tendencies, anger and sadness are seen as the direct opposites of wellbeing, and the feelings people should strive for, not only for themselves but also for their family and community (Alès, 2002). Similarly, for the Airo-Pai of Amazonian Peru, anger is perceived as a particularly dangerous force that spreads easily. Many efforts go into avoiding becoming angry and teaching children to fear anger. Behaviors that cause anger in the community are best avoided, so as not to stir it up in others, but so is an angry reaction in oneself, which should be controlled. Community wellbeing depends on cultivating the right kind of disposition in oneself and in children (Belaunde, 2000).

These Amazonian examples show us how fostering particular kinds of feelings in these contexts, and carefully cultivating emotional dispositions such as sympathy and equanimity, while nurturing these dispositions in others, is not only a crucial part of being and becoming a moral person: it is central to the art and craft of wellbeing. We can see here, too, how conviviality as a process typically involves more than relations with close kin (Killick, 2009; Santos-Granero, 2007). This is achieved through the careful cultivation of trust (Santos-Granero, 2007) and generosity, carefully taught even to very young children. Killick (2009) described the praise that parents were giving to their toddler whenever she was offering others food she had been given, even when she was taking it from her own mouth. Even though afraid and highly wary of outsiders, the Asheninka people with whom Killick worked offered him manioc beer, food, and a place to stay, displaying remarkable generosity at work. Undoubtedly, generosity and sharing food is one of the most widespread forms of conviviality in Amazonia and well beyond.

2.4 Bodies and Senses: Eating, Dancing, and Joking Together

Gathering and eating together, feasting, are important tools for conviviality in many places. The Latin roots of the word *convivium* refer to a feast or a banquet,[5]

---

hence the overtone of festive and joyful gathering in its current use in the English language.

Eating together is also considered an indispensable part of creating and maintaining social relationships in China. Ellen Oxfeld describes the friendly sociality and amicable atmosphere of shared meals in the rural Southeast. Meeting together and enjoying food in a group creates a liveliness known as *renao* – a bustling, noisy energy or festive feel, a quality considered important for gatherings. Even certain stages of serious or mournful events, such as funerals, might include gambling and food late into the night in order to offer a counterpoint to the loneliness of death (Oxfeld, 2017). Renao is sometimes translated as "red-hot sociality" (Chau, 2008), a term in which liveliness and heat are contrasted with sadness and loneliness. Temple markets, festivities, and family reunions are examples of such noisy, lively events, and children and grandchildren bring this quality of boisterous vitality into the everyday life of a household. This "hot" form of sociality is generally seen as desirable but can also, on occasion, be seen as unrefined or as linked to certain problematic behaviors, such as gambling (Steinmüller, 2011).

Oxfeld (2017) described another important aspect that eating together sometimes entails: rareness (*nande*). This quality might, for example, refer to a rare occasion, perhaps a rare visit of a long-absent family member or a friend from abroad. Rarity also refers to the special status of foods that might be difficult to acquire – vegetables grown in one's home village, perhaps, delivered by a visiting relative; or special delicacies (Oxfeld, 2017). Eating together can be used to strengthen and emphasize hierarchical relationships or more egalitarian bonds, depending on the event. In a more formal banquet, the host offers a lot of food and might take pride in providing something rare for the guests, all the while acting humble about the offerings. Guests might find it difficult to decline further offers of food, even when they are full. This led Oxfeld to contemplate the dynamic involved, whereby the host feels happy the more food the guest eats, with the hope that the shared joy will create an emotional bond and evoke feelings of familial closeness. Other events can be organized in a more egalitarian fashion, with no one in particular hosting the event. For example, in the making of a communal one-dish meal, neighbors might all contribute the ingredients and cook together in an informal atmosphere (Oxfeld, 2017).

While some foods are seen as better social conduits (Oxfeld, 2017), more appropriate for creating and sustaining a convivial atmosphere, the meaning of foods can differ widely. In Japan, fast food like hamburgers is often seen as more of a treat or a snack than as food for sustenance, or as a meal. It is also often shared and enjoyed communally in a similar way to other snacks (Traphagan & Brown, 2002). In other words, while fast food is served fast, it is not necessarily considered a fast way to get sustenance but often shared by families in a set of social events, which may be unfolding at a slower pace.

A recognition that eating together not only involves sharing but also entails a form of exchange underpins food sharing (commensality) as a principle of building relationships. Reciprocity in shared meals can be direct, when people take turns to host each other, or generalized, in cases where a range of more informal gifts circulates in a community without a clear account of who is a giver and who is a receiver, on the premise that the balance will even out over time. Intentional communities and cohousing projects in Canada and Japan, for example, take communal cooking and eating to be a central element of what constitutes living well together. Growing food, shopping and cooking, eating and cleaning up afterward all give opportunities for coming together and reaffirming the egalitarian and engaged ethos of the cohousing projects described by Catharine Kingfisher (2021).

Eating together, as a convivial practice, is also clearly an embodied practice aimed at creating closeness and intimacy. In the Amazonian context, close and intimate bonds are created through sharing food, often to the point that those involved are recognized as effectively becoming *of the same substance* (e.g., Vilaça, 2002). In other words, one becomes kin by eating together or estranged by eating apart. Yet eating is not the only embodied practice that can serve as a basis for conviviality. Consider, for instance, the practice of communal bathing in Japan (Clark, 2009). Until the 1970s, many Japanese houses did not have a bathroom on the premises, and neighborhood communal baths were abundant. Even now, bathing with others – friends, family members, and coworkers – Is not unusual, with the communal bathhouse offering a much-needed space for intimacy and sociality.

Another strength of conviviality as an approach to wellbeing, apart from the capacity to incorporate the political and ethical domains in explorations of mundane interactions, is its capacity to encompass the sensory alongside the embodied. Not only do we live together in an embodied fashion, but this sense of wellbeing alongside others can also be sensed. In other words, living well together can be induced and supported, as well as undermined, through particular senses. The smell of damp wool and unwashed overcoats on a packed commuter train might impose limits on a sense of wellbeing or convivial dwelling; on the other hand, certain sounds and smells might be very closely associated with living well together. For example, smells of certain festive dishes that are only cooked with family or a large group, might be familiar to many of us. Such is a smell of Polish *uszka* dumplings filled with mushrooms, which are only made for the Christmas Eve dinner in my family home – we only ever make them together. Another example might be the laughter and noise of children's voices, associated with the Chinese notion of *renao*, or red hot sociality, mentioned earlier, which encompasses the noisy and clamorous form of sociality.

Jamie Coates (2017) described conviviality within hairdressers' shops in Tokyo run and frequented by Chinese minority members. These spaces bring people together with some regularity, and as the rents are so high in Tokyo, the rooms are always small and busy, facilitating *renao*. Loud music and banter serve as an antidote to the loneliness that many recent immigrants or busy office workers feel (Coates, 2017). That such spaces are cheap and cramped is not insignificant, for much that comes with affluence and convenience does not necessarily facilitate social relationships; accidental and frequent contact and accidental connection have developed spontaneously over time. It also often has an environmental impact – consider home deliveries of food and shopping, that allow one to never venture into shops where one might meet someone; or supermarkets that sell everything, but do not require talking to a shopkeeper in the way that markets do. My own Japanese interlocutors in the merchant neighborhood of Osaka, especially older people, recognized the incredible convenience and ease of many of those amenities, but also the loneliness they might bring (see Kavedžija, in press).

Conviviality seems never to come without challenges. Di Nunzio (2019) wrote about the lives of young men growing up in Arada, the inner city area of Addis Ababa. He described Arada as not merely a place but a way of going through life (Di Nunzio, 2019). We could argue that Arada exemplifies both a locus and a modus of conviviality, one marked by challenge, conflict, and tension. In the space of social exclusion and marked socioeconomic differenti-ation, a young person is considered to "be Arada" when they embody a certain kind of personhood – smart, generous, and stylish (Di Nunzio, 2019). This kind of person is street smart, perhaps a bit of a trickster, but stands up in defense of others and is able to uphold social relationships with flair and style – again revealing how morality, politics, and aesthetics are interrelated.

A different set of challenges pervades the volatile conviviality of a Moscow market, a bazaar mostly attended by poorer inhabitants and characterized by neighborly sociality, albeit less stable and more dependent on seasons and working rhythms of sales (Nikolotov, 2019). The relationships between the vendors, not without tensions, are marked by amicable exchanges and banter, in which joking comprises an important convivial skill. "Sometimes male sellers and traders instigate pranks and hide each other's goods, causing the owner distress when they are tricked into believing that their merchandise has been stolen. In the case of the market sellers, though, it is sometimes difficult to ascertain whether a trick is an attack or a joke" (Nikolotov, 2019, p. 889).

Discerning the appropriate boundaries requires practice. In short, conviviality requires effort and skill, and is a continuous process rather than a state of harmony. Moreover, convivial practices are embodied, and play out in peoples' sensory worlds.

2.5 Conviviality in Diverse Urban Environments

Given that Amazonian groups are often relatively small and somewhat removed from the central institutions of the encompassing nation-state, one might argue that Amazonian groups are especially or unusually convivial (see Kohn, 2005). At the same time, one must recognize that communal harmony in Amazonian groups is often delicate and unstable for the same reason, as it might be less solidified in the form of social institutions. Conviviality can in fact be considered a helpful conceptual tool in a broad range of cultural settings, as it encapsulates the processual nature of the efforts and skills required to live well together. In other words, while the concept was developed within anthropology in relation to a specific cultural setting, I now want to show why it is well suited for understanding wellbeing in a variety of very different contexts.

Conviviality has been adopted as a lens for studying everyday relationships between people of different backgrounds in super-diverse cities, as a counterbalance to the previously predominant ideas of multiculturalism and cosmopolitanism. For the most part, the focus in this work is on spontaneous, occasional, light, and loose senses of amicability among coexisting groups in cities such as London (Tyler, 2017). In the highly diverse London borough of Hackney, interactions in many public places indicate some degree of engagement, but also a certain distance and avoidance of potential sources of tension (Wessendorf, 2014). Interactions across cultural, ethnic, and racial lines sometimes lead to relationships of trust and care, as shown by Tyler (2017); however, they can simultaneously coexist with racist and xenophobic sentiments.

Some recent work has shown that, as a superficial phenomenon entailing friendly relations, conviviality does not preclude racism, exclusion, or violence. How can we even speak of conviviality, then, when even the more enduring convivial relations sometimes end in breakdown or violence? With reference to complex relations of community policing in Johannesburg, Vigneswaran (2014) argued that tense and even violent relations coexist in the same space as convivial exchanges and relationships. The author suggested that this radical case helps us understand the limits of conviviality, but I think it reveals something that is instead at the concept's very core. It is worth remembering that the use of the concept by anthropologists originated in the context of Amazonian groups whose interactions are often characterized by war, fighting, violence, and tension. It is in this context that an understanding of conviviality as living well with others emerges as something always ongoing: an imperfect process, relying on effort and skill, and an art form.

Unsurprisingly, migration studies tend to focus on diverse groups living together. However, this context can sometimes inadvertently narrow the conceptualization of conviviality. Magdalena Nowicka (2020), one of the scholars whose work initiated the use of conviviality in migration studies, recently reflected critically on its current use in the field. She pointed out that a focus on spaces marked by international migration effectively reduces conviviality to a set of skills for peaceful cohabitation, a description of living together that is somewhat superficial or thin, precluding real discussion of the complexities of power relations and the larger institutional contexts of exclusion and exploitation (Nowicka, 2020). Concerned that usage of the concept is mostly drawing attention to public spaces marked by a high degree of international migration, Nowicka suggested a more experience-near or phenomenological approach in order to flesh out intimate experiences while also attending to inequalities and challenges and the affective qualities of living together. Which, in turn, brings us back to the notions of political emotions and moral moods (such as fear, anger, or anxiety over aging; see Kavedžija, 2016), as attention to the affective qualities of experiences of living together forms the basis for an understanding of a life together that is at once intimate and political.

To summarize, then, one problem with current uses of conviviality as a framing device in the literature on migration is how it foregrounds particular relations of difference, notably ethnicity and culture, and inadvertently reifies them. One solution, instead of focusing on skills for living well with ethnically or culturally "other" neighbors, is to consider the skills for living well with more inclusively conceived persons. This allows us to move away from bounded groups and might also be helpful to expand our frame of reference beyond clearly bounded individuals. It is important not to treat societies as constituted of relatively autonomous individuals but as people who are always already interdependent and mutually constituted. As such, for a successful link between conviviality and wellbeing, it is important to link it to care, which I will discuss in detail in the following section. Moving away from an understanding of conviviality as a tool for analyzing cohabitation of ethnically or culturally diverse groups alongside one another allows us to consider the techniques for living well together as encompassing a broad range of others, including nonhumans such as plants, animals, objects, and other features of the surrounding environment.

2.6 More-Than-Human Conviviality

Conviviality, at its best, draws our attention to the fact that wellbeing is not only social but *deeply relational*. It is not merely an evaluation of one's own life, nor does it unfold within the enclosed body of a lone individual. Rather, it plays out in relationship with one's surrounding environment: with tools and technologies, with materials, with human and nonhuman beings. It matters how we think about our relationships with these other entities; not least, it matters for how we interact with them, as it frames our perceptions and expectations. These in turn can have a profound impact on our wellbeing. The way we conceive of these relationships affects others in turn, and their wellbeing and health, which in turn reflects on us. Thus, witnessing the suffering of others, for instance, or inhabiting a deteriorating environment, is likely to affect us negatively.

Relationships with other species, and an approach to our own lives as a multispecies existence, have become a topic of much discussion and interest of late. The lives of all kinds of other species, from animals and plants to fungi and beyond, are entwined in multiple ways with human social and cultural existence (Kirksey & Helmreich, 2010). One of the most obvious ways is our coexistence with, and reliance on, domesticated animals such as pets. Herders and farmers in various places have a close relationship with their cattle (Donati, 2019); people form close bonds with elephants (Locke, 2017), forests (Kohn, 2013), and fungi (Tsing, 2015), to name but a few species entanglements. What does it ultimately mean to say our own existence, as humans, is a multispecies existence? Human bodies are far from impervious or autonomous units, separate from other beings: just think of how we rely on the microbiome in our gut and are increasingly aware of the complex effects of microorganisms on our evolution.

> You, like me, probably think of yourself as a human being. You sense and experience your body as a human body, with luck having two legs, two arms, a brain, and what have you, all composed of tissues and organs made up of human cells. Moreover, you conceive of yourself as a distinct individual. Wrong. Your body is teeming with alien life-forms. It turns out that you harbor within your body whole populations of nonhumans that have separate DNA structures to you, and they outnumber you. (Stern, 2020, p. 254)

The understanding that our own bodies are symbiotic systems (Eloe-Fadrosh & Rasko, 2013; Stern, 2020) makes living well and artfully with others an even more crucial aspect of wellbeing. This extends to what we might otherwise think of as "the environment." Research shows that spending time in outdoor spaces has a beneficial effect on wellbeing and stress recovery (Corazon et al., 2019). As such, it is certainly not inconceivable that places that appear under strain – certain places of ruin, say (Navaro-Yashin, 2012) – might have a negative effect on our wellbeing. In many cultures, the entities in the surrounding world are considered deserving a proper treatment, consideration, and respect.

Let us consider a rather radical example: a stone. Stones are usually thought of as impassive and unchanging, and yet – departing from a moving description of a particular stone in Norway, named Stallo, with enduring cultural significance – the anthropologist Hugo Reinert (2016) proposed a change in research attitudes together with a different imaginary way for relating to stones, and to what is usually obscured by an animate-inanimate, binary way of thinking. Over the years, Stallo has been used as a Sami sacrifice stone, and many considered it powerful in a sense that we might label metaphysical, although most everyday interactions with it resemble a more ordinary, polite neighborliness. One of Reinert's interlocutors in the field, a reindeer herder, observed that one should stop and attend to the stone when passing nearby, simply because it is polite to acknowledge another upon encountering them – be they a human, a reindeer, or a stone. Stallo the stone also finds itself in a resource-rich environment, thus attractive for extraction, which appears unproblematic when viewed from a perspective that favors the economy, which prioritizes humans, and within which the stone is merely a cultural and historical artifact. Yet the relational mode of thinking of many local inhabitants imbues respect for the stone, and for other nonhuman entities, with an ethical character: understanding them as beings that can be harmed (Reinert, 2016). Dwelling on the words of the writer Ursula Le Guin, "Subjectify the universe – because look where objectifying has got us," Reinert ends with an invitation to think of nonhuman entities as subjects, rather than as objects to be subjugated, used, or exploited.

Our attitudes toward the nonhuman entities that surround us must change if we wish to feel well and live better than we do. If we adopt a conviviality perspective on wellbeing, one that is capacious and includes more-than-human conviviality, it becomes clear that to live well, we need to cultivate healthy relationships with others. Exploitative relationships rather than relations of nurturance and care are neither sustainable nor healthy, and while undoubtedly harmful to the subjugated party, they cannot be considered conducive to the wellbeing of the dominating party. In other words, subjective wellbeing is incomplete without consideration of our relationships with all those others that surround us, or, even more radically, without considering them as part of ourselves, since we are constituted through multiple relations of care – as the following section will make clear.

2.7 Convivial Distance

When scholars write about sociality, they do not always engage the same set of concerns. In their discussion of this concept, Long and Moore (2013) warned against the often unspoken, underlying assumptions of what sociality ought to entail (see also Anderson, 2015). Heeding their warning, I should be wary of analytical vagueness. Moreover, we must avoid the pitfalls of drawing assumptions about conviviality based on the particular practices it may involve in some contexts. What is seen as convivial, and valued as a form of living well in one place, is not necessarily equally valued elsewhere – nor should it be. In order to encompass a plethora of different ways of living well, a convivial approach must acknowledge the challenges that it presents and the efforts required to craft it. Living well together should certainly not always be understood as loud or vivacious, say, or even as actively engaged.

If conviviality is to be understood in its broadest sense as living well with others, then it must encompass all kinds of ways of being together – not only active engagement but also more subtle forms of life-in-common. It is important to point out, therefore, that conviviality should not imply something like "facing one another." Other forms of involvement and copresence may be just as important: working alongside someone, gardening, walking or driving together, making things together or alongside others.[6] It may be fruitful to expand this line of thinking to encompass engagement that is less direct – not focused on another being, that is, but oriented toward a shared task or activity. An "alongside" orientation, we might say, rather than "across," or "facing one another," is an important aspect of many convivial practices and often highly conducive for wellbeing.

Living well together can also entail a certain amount of distance from others: space or time apart. This disengagement from relationship, or from common activities, might take the form of solitary time, whether spontaneous or structured. Even in the cultural contexts in which being together is highly valued, some time might be given over to stepping away from one's usual duties or activities. In those places where sleeping right through the night is not the norm, one's night-time wakefulness might be used as a time for private reflection. Throughout history, in many parts of the world, women have been required to withdraw socially and rest during their menstruation (e.g., Glowczewski, 2019).[7] Margaret Mead and Gregory Bateson documented in their visual ethnography the dynamics of engagement and withdrawal among the inhabitants of Bali. On the one hand, they documented crowds and rituals featuring music and dance. On the other hand, they presented various forms of disengaging from others, stepping back from social relationships, from the task at hand, from the

---

[6] This is what Jackson refers to as dia-praxis, in opposition to dia-logue (Jackson, 2019).

[7] That does not always mean that women are alone during this time, as several women might be spending time together in seclusion, in which case this might end up being quite a sociable and lively encounter, at times entailing song and dance (see Gottlieb, 2002).

sensory engagements. The photographs presented in these sections include apparently daydreaming children, disengagement at the end of the trance dance, an artisan staring into space after completing a piece of work, exhausted (Bateson & Mead, 1942; see also Jackson, 2012).

Detachment, though neglected by many anthropological accounts, is very much desired, particularly in contexts that involve intense social ties, as Candea and his colleagues (Candea et al., 2015) argued. The acts of crafting and severing relations are best seen as connected and inseparable, as Strathern (1996) made clear in her work on kinship in Melanesia. More active forms of detachment, such as ascetic practices, are often seen from the outside as dependent upon a range of social relationships (Cook, 2015). Yet detachment should not be seen merely as a supportive mechanism for sociality; it must be understood in its own right. The importance of periods of detachment for wellbeing is considerable, particularly when fostering reflection and creativity – as discussed in more detail in the final section.

To summarize, to the extent that wellbeing is best understood as living well with others, it relies on both active engagement and the possibility, at least, for various forms of withdrawal, be they physical or mental. While togetherness might be most highly valued in those contexts sometimes described (though not unproblematically) as "socio-centric," detachment remains very important in those places also. Even if physical detachment is neither possible nor desired, then a certain form of mental privacy might be sought. In the context of the Amazonian Urarina, Walker described an unwillingness to speculate on thoughts and motivations of others – a tendency also found in many Oceanic peoples (see Robbins & Rumsey, 2008). Although much of their daily life is conducted in the open view of other villagers – as Urarina houses have roofs but no walls – Walker's (2020) interlocutors generally refused to answer apparently straightforward questions such as, for instance, "Why do you think that Ignacio got up in the middle of the conversation like that?" Instead of offering a guess, the answer would be something like, "Oh, you'd have to ask him!" In such a context, detachment can become a priority. As Walker put it: "In immediate social environments like this, close proximity to others is a given, to the extent that people can all too easily feel like their personal boundaries are being eroded. Connecting with others is easy; differentiation, on the other hand, must be actively affirmed" (Walker, 2020, p. 154).

Similarly, living together well and harmoniously with others might, in many places, be seen as requiring a certain degree of social distance. For example, the older Japanese with whom I worked were finding themselves increasingly isolated in the changing urban landscape. They sought connection, but were all too aware that they do not wish to recreate the "sticky" neighborhood ties of the past, as these often left little privacy – people knew what you were doing, when, and with whom, they told me. As they aged, and their friends passed away, they recognized the need to form new relationships. I met most of them in a community salon, an open café-like space in the neighborhood. One of the women in charge of running the volunteer-staffed salon told me:

> [We are doing this] so that people wouldn't become isolated, live somewhat spaced out, private . . . [But] You see, while hedgehogs might want to pile up for warmth, they might also feel uncomfortable when they are too close together. Being too close can create annoying relationships (*okorisuru yōna kankei*), so we want to create a place where people can cordially live together (*minna de nakayoku kurashite*) while still maintaining a sense of distance (*kyōrikan*). That is our purpose. (Kavedžija, 2019, p. 2)

Manners, doing things properly, well and with attention, treating others with attention, and considering their feelings, were all seen as important for creating and maintaining social relationships. We often have a tendency to see politeness and manners, or a careful attention to "form," as associated with distancing and demarcating boundaries between groups. Aware of this, my interlocutors remained ever mindful of possibilities for social divisions, and used politeness as a way of lubricating social encounters. Remaining aware of the need of others for their own time and space, they tried to look out for each other, but without keeping an eye on each other at all times (Kavedžija, 2019). In other words, some polite distance served as a convivial tool, a practice of "doing things properly," allowing them to create new social ties in later life.

2.8 Convivial Wellbeing: Arts of Living Together

In conclusion, conviviality foregrounds arts of living together. It acknowledges the ongoing and processual nature of living with others, as well as the challenging nature of this life together. In short, conviviality requires and entails effort, art, and skill. Living well together is an ongoing endeavor, and the skills favored in particular places are taught and fostered in the context of relations of care. Conviviality brings together political and moral, affective and aesthetic domains of living in the world. Convivial practices may include joking, banter, eating together, working together, celebrations and festivities, and dance and music. Living well with others, furthermore, encompasses various orientations: facing one another and standing by, working or walking along. It relies on the skillful balancing of engagement and disengagement, coming together and moving apart, being caught up (in an activity or a group) and stepping back (separating physically or withdrawing to reflect).

Conviviality draws attention to the embodied nature of living with others, including people similar to and different from us, nonhuman animals and other entities in the environment. It involves objects and technologies, as well as natural entities that surround us. More-than-human conviviality is ever more important in the current context of the Anthropocene. People in various cultural settings have incorporated a broad range of practices for living with others into their daily lives, such as giving thanks, showing respect, and attending to the places from which they receive their food, nourishment, and shelter. It is not inconceivable that our current mental health crisis, the proliferation of various forms of mental health concerns, is intertwined with our witnessing of large-scale suffering, neglect, disrespect, and abandonment of humans and nonhumans around us. Treating mental health as internal and as pertaining to the individual may be inadequate for addressing these kinds of concerns, which are better understood as affective ecologies of health.

3 Care

Care is a crucial part of human relationships and interactions. It is a fundamental human practice: it would not be exaggerating to say that care is what makes us human. In the words of Arthur Kleinman (2009): "[C]aregiving is a defining moral practice . . . that makes caregivers, and at times even care receivers, more present and therefore more fully human" (p. 293). Kleinmann's discussion of care highlights its ubiquity and its relational nature. Indeed, as humans, we come into the world reliant on the care of others rather than as autonomous individuals. Care can be found in the public and private spheres, in domestic as much as institutional settings. It can be nurturing and rewarding, but also taxing or burdensome; a gift and form of labor, and sometimes both at once. As a moral practice, care has the potential to make us better people; however, it can also be entwined with a range of more ambivalent processes linked to abandonment, disregard, or outright evil (Biehl, 2012). We must therefore be careful not to romanticize care or view it in necessarily positive terms: it is entangled with medical, technical, and institutional regimes in complex ways, the effects of which can be supportive but also cruel or ambiguous.

In what ways, then, can care be helpful for understanding wellbeing? I will explore the integrative aspects of care and its capacity to bring together the ethical and the political, the intimate and the public spheres, closer together. I will draw on ideas from the feminist ethics of care and a range of anthropological sources to expand the meaning of care as a practice and as a disposition. I argue that care is fundamental for wellbeing because it constitutes the very subjects that experience it. Care is constitutive of the ties and relationships that constitute humans (and nonhumans) as subjects, capable of experiencing subjective wellbeing.

"Tell me your cares and I will tell you who you are!" In her moving ethnography of care for her mother with dementia, Janelle Taylor (2008) used her mother's phrase – a reminder and an exhortation to "keep the cares together" – as an invitation to reframe what matters most in our relations with those for whom we care, be they dementia patients or otherwise. Rather than focusing on memory (and recognition) as the core of personhood, she described situations in which her mother showed care for her and pointed to how this is an equally important, if not more fundamental, quality. Care is fundamental to our existence and sense of self – we care about and care for people, living beings, environments, things, and ideas. Care is not merely relevant to wellbeing, it is the maintenance of wellbeing itself.

3.1 Practices of Care

[C]aring can be viewed as a species activity that includes everything that we do to maintain, continue, and repair our "world" so that we can live in it as well as possible. That world includes our bodies, our selves, and our environment, all of which we seek to interweave in a complex, life-sustaining web.

(Tronto & Fisher, 1990, p. 40)

While much work on care in medical anthropology and sociology focuses on healthcare settings, I am interested in care in a broader sense, as a practice that extends to a broad range of human (and more-than-human) relationships. In an attempt to explore health beyond the medical sphere, Emily Yates-Doerr and Megan Carney (2016) focused on the kitchen as a site of care in the family and in the community. Care in the kitchen is a relational practice, as the women in six Latin-American kitchens that formed the main field sites for the research did not focus on individuals but on the meals:

[T]hey did not identify an individualized or medicalized subject to whom care is directed or in whom health resides. By caring for and through food, women attended to the immediate event of the meal, to the histories from which the meal emerged, and to the futures it would help to produce. The health they sought to nourish was dispersed across collectives and time (Yates-Doerr & Carney, 2016, p. 5).

By carefully attending to food, the Latin-American women in this study exemplified care as an embodied practice. Furthermore, they were nurturing relationships of care – the meals are shared, eaten together, and encompass more than one person or body at a time. This provides us with a good example of wellbeing as relational and social rather than individual.

The practice of care is not apolitical or removed from relations of power. For example, Adam Drazin (2011) described a range of housework practices in Romania, focused around cleaning, some of which are so intense and sustained that he described them as "aggressive" (p. 500). Appearing clean and well groomed is contrasted with the neglect evident in some institutional settings (such as dilapidated official buildings), resulting in practices that Drazin described as "smothering in love" (p. 501). However, the burden of care weighs differently on different household members. Moreover, such embodied care is not simply related to wellbeing in any straightforward way because an excess of care can be – and sometimes is – experienced as oppressive. In what follows, I will focus on relations of care as a basis for constitution of "subjects" of subjective wellbeing.

3.2 Subjects of Care

It is sometimes tempting to imagine human endeavors as carried out between independent and autonomous individuals who are both rational and largely self-sufficient. In that vision, "society" or the social tends to be explained in terms of competition or collaboration between enclosed and bounded entities. Yet things look different if one sees human lives as fundamentally interdependent and entwined from the outset: that people are always already dependent on others, continually receiving and providing care. In this view, collaboration and rationality do not emerge from already formed individuals; instead, collaboration as interdependency brings persons into being. It could be argued that not only is care necessary to nurture a person and bring it to life, but that ongoing caring relationships constitute persons. Feminist work on care places an emphasis on relationships and rejects claims that moral reasoning is impersonal, and best grounded in abstract principles. In her influential text *In a Different Voice*, Carol Gilligan (1993 [1982]) contested the prevailing ideas of moral development in children, which pointed to the findings that boys reach moral maturity earlier than girls by attaining command of impersonal moral principles. Instead, she argued for the need to rethink what constitutes moral maturity, by moving away from impersonal abstract principles and considering the specific social and relational context.

> Moral maturity is a strongly care-oriented perspective, an ethical attitude toward individual others, a community, and the world – as well as, importantly, oneself. Awareness of and attention to one's own rights and needs and to those of others inform this attitude, which entails seeing oneself as part of a couple, a family, a community – but it does not mean subordinating one's own wishes and rights to what seems best for those larger social units. (Hauskeller, 2020, p. 156)

The ethics of care, then, directs our attention to the moral and ethical significance of the relationships of care that constitute our worlds, based on a recognition that human beings depend on others throughout their lives for support and emotional wellbeing. Not only is care in this context seen as one of the defining human characteristics, the very primacy of care highlights its importance and urgency. Held (2006, p. 11) argued that care is "pressing," not least for those who depend on it. In this sense, "An ethics of care directs our attention to the need for responsiveness in relationships (paying attention, listening, responding)," Gilligan said in a 2011 interview. I take the concept of care to be both a practice and an attitude, a disposition that can be cultivated and expanded – a point I expand further in the text in relation to wellbeing.

Allow me to return to the well-known definition by Tronto and Fischer, cited in the epigraph of this section, as it warrants a closer look: "[C]aring can be viewed as a species activity that includes everything that we do to maintain, continue, and repair our 'world' so that we can live in it as well as possible. That world includes our bodies, our selves, and our environment, all of which we seek to interweave in a complex, life-sustaining web" (1990, p. 40). In this definition, care is clearly related to wellbeing because it is fundamental to its realization: care is required to live well; it is what we do; what we give and receive. Feminist thought on care distinguishes two entwined aspects of care: care about and care for (Tronto, 1998). A similar distinction has been made between care as a value and care as a practice (Held, 2006). Caring *for* orients our attention to something and someone that requires care and is about the recognition of needs. As not all needs are seen as equally pressing, not all needs are always given equal attention. What we care *about* is closely related to values, which naturally vary across social and cultural contexts.

The feminist ethics of care is sometimes presented as an antidote to normative moral reasoning based on abstract principles and ideals. While care is here understood as a value and a practice, it is also defined in normative terms: what constitutes good care is articulated and analyzed, and there is an attempt to identify the qualities and characteristics of a good caring person. Held asserted that a caring person cares with the right kind of attitude or "appropriate motivations"; they need to respond to the needs of others and to provide care in a competent way (Held, 2006, p. 4). Although broadly supported by many anthropological accounts of care, some aspects of this normative ideal of a caring person are nevertheless called into question by close anthropological investigations, especially in non-Western contexts of care. For example, Felicity Aulino (2019) described family carers in Thailand as oriented toward care as a practice that should be performed repeatedly, reliably, and correctly.

For carers and family members alike, good care was care well performed. Very little emphasis was placed on cultivating the right kind of attitude toward care, in terms of inner motivations or intentions (Aulino, 2019). Although there was a preference overall for equanimity and calm, sometimes daughters experienced frustration and other negative emotions while caring, but this did not mean that the care they provided was bad or that they were bad daughters. What mattered most was that they performed the care, regardless of any inner turmoil. They were seen to be good daughters simply because they did the right things. In this sense, care was not unlike a ritual, which is primarily about practice (Aulino, 2012), but perhaps also in the sense that participating in a ritual can in fact also affect one's emotions and inner dispositions. Doing something can change how we feel, and performing care can be such a transformative practice, cultivating feelings of closeness.

Perhaps the most important lesson to be taken from the feminist ethics of care is the need to focus on relationships when understanding personhood. That is, persons should not be seen as independent or distinct from the relationships in which they are embedded; they are created, supported, and maintained through their relationships of care. Caring is a way of ensuring and furthering the wellbeing of the cared-for, the recipient of care, but also that of the carer. Care can sometimes be laborious but is not merely one directional. A focus on care transcends the issues of altruism versus self-interest (Held, 2006); at its best, it is both at once. Care is integrative and can, at its best, improve the wellbeing of both sides. While it does require considering the needs of the givers and the recipients of care (when such sides are articulated), and these can come in conflict or tension, care can be seen as enmeshed with wellbeing of both. No matter what, care is relational in the sense that it focuses our attention on relationships. I argue that as a conceptual framework, care allows us to move from merely stating that wellbeing has a social component to understanding the relational quality of wellbeing. So, when we attend to subjective wellbeing of others, why do we still ask, "How do you feel? On a scale of 1–10, how happy are you?" We might well ask instead: "What are your cares? Who and what do you care about, and care for? What care do you receive?"

3.3 States of Care

If care for those who depend on us is pressing (meaning, both urgent and vital), as Held (2006) reminded us, then understanding relations of care is paramount if we seek to explore questions of responsibility. Whom do we consider responsible for wellbeing – does the responsibility lie with the state, with the community, with the family, or with the individual? Many contemporary discourses on wellbeing and happiness tend to locate responsibility with the individual. As the Latin proverb would have it, *faber est quisque fortunae suae*, every person is the maker of their own fortune. This stance can be empowering, as it might offer the individual a sense of agency, but if the problems they are facing are structural and relational, these circumstances and obstacles cannot be addressed by the individual alone. The framework of care shifts focus to the relational nature of wellbeing and opens new possibilities for understanding responsibility.

Considering the wellbeing and health of entire populations brings with it a range of problems. Which parts of the population should be included, and who falls outside of the purview of any given organization or government? Are state borders to be considered boundaries of care? Is everyone within the population to be treated equally? These issues, and more, come to the fore when governments, policy makers, and international organizations consider wellbeing of populations (see also Bok, 2010). One example of thinking of wellbeing in terms of populations can be found in Didier Fassin's (2008) work on humanitarian reasons. In his discussion of changes in immigration policies in France, Fassin traced the changes in the reasoning and rationale for approving asylum for some immigrants while continuing to deny it to many others, treating most applicants as potentially unlawful immigrants. Fassin showed how, rather than recognizing the rights of immigrants or an obligation for their care as persons, justifications hinge on humanitarian reasoning rather than political status alone. For example, he described the grueling case of a young woman, orphaned earlier in her life and subjected to rape, whose right to asylum would not have been accepted on the grounds of her mental health. Yet when it transpires she is HIV positive and treatment is not available in her country of origin, the claim is recognized on humanitarian grounds: "What she had not been able to get as a right had finally been given to her by compassion" (Fassin, 2008, p. 368).

That some situations make some people more in need of our care is not without consequence, as Fassin made clear. In practice, sadly, in many societies (including in France), not all lives are valued equally. Yet as these actions are justified in terms of acting on a principle of humanitarian reason and alleviating the suffering of some, the citizens and the governments of those societies can continue believing that they are acting morally: "For humanitarian government does more than just preserve our conception of the human: through the moral sense it credits us with, it endows us with our own share of humanity" (Fassin, 2011, p. 271). By focusing on particular forms of suffering, the regimes of care in question construct a particular vision of morality and personhood, at odds with the claims of universal "humanity."

As Ticktin (2011) described in her book *Casualties of Care*, the recourse to humanitarian reason casts those who qualify as exceptions rather than as people with rights. Regardless of their motivations to alleviate suffering, Ticktin argued that these "regimes of care" prevent the possibility of more systemic and broad-ranging action. Such change could involve extending support and rights to those whose situation is difficult due to poverty or labor exploitation, which are not recognized as sufficient grounds to warrant asylum. Therefore, while aimed at the relief of suffering, the politics of care in this context hinges on an understanding of suffering dominated by medicalized definitions. This particular understanding of suffering, as focused on bodies, tends to be presented, in scientific terms, as objective and universal (Ticktin, 2011). Yet, rather than universal, it is mediated and politically and socially framed.[8]

The way care is politically framed, and used as a justification or discourse, is thus not straightforward or unproblematic. How care is defined – in this instance as the alleviation of particular forms of suffering – includes some people and excludes others. In different contexts, however, a government might seek to extend care to its populations in an impersonal fashion, guided by a principle of fairness. Writing about two cases of care for Inuit in the Arctic, Lisa Stevenson (2014) described *anonymous care* – blindly and evenly offered to anyone, without regard to who they are. This lack of regard may appear uncaring, or worse, to those over whom it extends: "[I]t often seems to make no difference for whom the state cares. Such indifference is sometimes perceived by Inuit as uncaring, even at times murderous, though it is always couched by the state in terms of benevolence and concern" (Stevenson, 2014, p. 4). In the context of tuberculosis treatment in the 1960s and the current suicide intervention programs in the Canadian Arctic, the focus is firmly trained on the preservation of life. For those who are taken away from their communities and hospitalized far away from home, with barely any contact with their loved ones, as was the case for many Inuit with tuberculosis in the past, such care for life may feel unbearable or inhumane.

Another discussion of care and life can be found in the work of Jarret Zigon (2018). Describing programs for drug users in the United States and Canada, Zigon sharply contrasted the anonymous nature of care focused on life, defined in biopolitical terms, with what he terms *attuned care*, attentive to the person in the present moment. Caring must be more than merely trying to preserve lives, for "with the contemporary dominance of biopolitics, this

---

[8] What Ticktin aims to do is to explore the place of care and its uses in the context of politics. "By invoking a politics of care, I mean to address the central place of benevolence and compassion in contemporary political life, especially when enacted under the threat of emergency" (Ticktin, 2010, p. 3).

caring-for and taking-care-of life has too often become a process of normalization rather than an attunement to the singularity of whoever arrives" (Zigon, 2018, p. 134). Not unlike Stevenson, Zigon showed that this political and biopolitical understanding of care portrays life as life in general, instead of considering lives of any particular person or persons. In contrast, attuned care does not make assumptions about the common nature of life or suffering, instead focusing on specificities of what is needed and what kind of life is being encountered. It is open and responsive, allowing someone to be who and what they are (Zigon, 2018). Care, at its bests, resists the impersonal, as it is always directed toward something and someone. It is not possible to conceive of care entirely in the abstract because care is what makes the person concrete, it is relational, and it brings persons about.

3.4 Labor of Love

Although care is undoubtedly a moral practice, it also is or can be a form of work. Erdmute Alber and Heike Drotbohm (2015) argued for an understanding of care as work closely related to kinship ties and inflected by movement through the life course. Kin care for one another, but care can also create close bonds to replace or supplement kinship. In terms of life course, they argued that not only do different life stages require different levels of care, but some are also framed by the responsibility for the care of others. In other words, life stages might be defined by specific obligations to give and/or to receive care. In this sense, care is best understood as bringing together various aspects of life with others: work, kinship and life course, that might have previously been studied separately (Alber & Drotbohm, 2015). Consider housework and cooking, or care for the children and the elders: it is at once a form of work and a form of family ration, kinship, in which duties and obligations shift according to the life stage – for instance, a mother who cared for children might receive support from them in older age.

Feminist and Marxist scholars highlight the nature of care as work (Alber & Drotbohm, 2015) that may involve emotional labor (Hochschild, 2012) or the performance of particular emotions. The labor of care is a sensory and embodied labor. In her research with home helpers for the elderly in Chicago, Elana Buch (2013) examined the wide-ranging sensory involvement of carers in their clients' worlds. In one situation she described, for instance, an older client is transported to a hospital with a gastrointestinal infection, and the carer responds by rushing to dispose of all the milk in the refrigerator. The carer would smell the opened milk regularly, compensating for her older client's weakening sense of smell and taste, and while she could have replaced milk with a more durable beverage, she chose instead to support the client's habits by drawing upon her own senses. Yet while carers would routinely support the sensory worlds of their clients – by cooking familiar foods, for example – there was no similar expectation that the clients would aim to attend to the senses of the helpers, implying the existence of certain sensory and embodied hierarchies. "The labor of caregiving generates more than novel forms of morality and personhood," argued Buch (2013, p. 638), "it also generates and reproduces systematic, intersecting forms of structural inequality." Whether remunerated or not, care often figures as a form of work, but the way it is perceived and evaluated by both the caregiver and care receiver is often not straightforward.

It is not necessarily the case that institutional or paid care is "cold," or that care by close family members is necessarily preferable, or "warm." In many cases, the care provided by paid carers in institutional contexts can be very attentive, intimate, and cordial, not to mention perceived in positive terms by carers and care recipients alike. Similarly, under strain, family carers might suffer, and stories of neglect are not infrequent. Such situations are often described in terms of "misplaced" care, argued Tatiana Thelen (2015, p. 510), who suggested that equating family care with authenticity and intimacy, and institutional care with efficiency and impersonality, is problematic. Instead of considering amiable and intimate institutional care (or distant and strained family care) as forms of misplaced care, these particular configurations of care deserve our full attention in their own right, as they give us a better insight into the social organization (Thelen, 2015). Attending to care allows us to trace the outline of social relations.

3.5 Communities of Care: Beyond Binary Care Relations

If care is generative and supports social relationships, it can also come under strain. The dynamic of care giving and care receiving is unequal. If understood as dyadic, this can cause strain, as the two parties, the caregiver and the care receiver, might not be in an equal position to care for one another. Of course, sometimes dependent elders or even small children show and enact care for their carers, and such care may not be experienced as a burden. Yet, when we speak of a dynamic between a caregiver and a recipient of care, what appears to emerge is a form of exchange that can be seen as asymmetrical. Instead, I suggest moving beyond this dyadic focus on care.

In my own research with older Japanese living in the city of Osaka, I traced a variety of relations of care (Kavedžija, 2016, 2019, 2020). While filial piety, which entails support for aging relatives, is still a strong family value in Japan, many of my older interlocutors worried about becoming increasingly in need of help and support and eventually becoming a burden on their children. If the media often portrayed younger generations as not sufficiently caring, it was often the elders who decided not to rely too much on the care from their children. Instead, they cultivated multiple networks of support and numerous caring relationships: in the community, with neighbors, with peers, with community organizations staffed by volunteers, or with local government care providers, drawing on a range of informal and more formal sources of support. Some older people dedicated much of their time to community volunteering, and several worked as home helpers for those in need. Many elders were variously involved in relations of care, looking out for one another, providing information, and helping others to organize small daily tasks, such as arranging a visit to the dentist or recommending a hairdresser. Unlike the communities of the past, they did not expect these small deeds to be reciprocated, even though that might have been expected in times past, when any small favor might need to be acknowledged with a gift, for instance.

Such circulation of favors and gifts in a tightly knit community was now considered somewhat intrusive and onerous among my older friends, and, as such, they did not romanticize the more enmeshed neighborhoods of the "olden times." Instead, in the spirit of community volunteering, they hoped to create a functioning community they could rely on themselves, should the need arise. Rather than expecting reciprocation, in other words, they implied that a community of care, with multiple relations of support, offered a degree of reassurance that help and care would come their way when needed. Furthermore, there was an understanding that various forms of care work in interconnected ways: looking after elders and looking after children required looking after mothers, who were often the carers for both. The older volunteers supported parents by looking after a community house, mostly used as a play space for children and a meeting space for parents, for instance. They enjoyed the company of young children, and the space offered considerable respite for the local parents. Good care, in this sense, is care that flows and circulates. It relies on several links and leaves no dead ends, where caregivers find themselves unsupported, overburdened, exhausted or isolated, or perhaps even suicidal (see Danely, 2017; O'Dwyer et al., 2016). Care is at its best in circulation, between people in numerous distributed and ongoing bonds. It might be asymmetrical and difficult to reciprocate when seen as an isolated, dyadic relationship between caregiver and care receiver, but when considered instead as a broader network of relationships, it provides carers with numerous links of support to more than one person.

When this enmeshed nature of care becomes visible, then it becomes clear that aiming wellbeing interventions and services at an individual emerges as at best partial. Instead, attending to networks and communities of care, we can perhaps locate the weak and the isolated. Often support is an entirely other part of the network of relationships of care is required. In the case of Japan, it may be that underpaid, overworked youth need support in order for the elderly to thrive. Perhaps, then, to expand eldercare, more should be invested in childcare and worker rights. Attending to specific communities of care opens up a different pathway to wellbeing, or indeed, numerous pathways.

What appears to be particularly important here is the understanding of care not as a dyadic relationship but also as enmeshing people in broader networks. Parenthood, for example, can pose considerable strain for working parents, but the distribution of responsibility and broader support from others in the family and community can transform this experience by providing invaluable support and care for the parent-carer. Two things become apparent from these discussions of care – that the relations of care are fundamental but need not be dyadic; and that care can be supportive but also exhausting for both parties, and a source of strain as much as wellbeing or fulfillment. At its best, though, care teaches us that strain, challenge, and effort are not in direct opposition to wellbeing. While neglect, abandonment, and disregard indicate insufficient and inadequate care, and are hence clearly at odds with wellbeing and human flourishing, they can also be seen as detrimental for self-realization and destructive for moral personhood of those who are in some ways responsible for the care of others. Disregard, in other words, may have consequences for those who do not (adequately) care. This point cannot be stressed enough: when one does not have the capacity to care for others, one's own wellbeing is at stake, too.

3.6 Care and Choice

We can learn much about care by contrasting it with other social processes and ideals. In her research on people living with diabetes, Annemarie Mol (2008, p. 8) contrasted what she called a "logic of care" and a "logic of choice," as two different sets of meanings and "modes of ordering" that underpin practices in various domains of life, especially health care. Mol took a critical look at the ideal of patient choice, which is implicitly linked with an understanding of the patient as primarily an individual. Choice acquires a particular meaning in the neoliberal context of consumer choice, which frames freedom primarily as the freedom to choose, preferable to lack of choice or force. At the same time, one can only choose from what is on offer: between products that are conceptualized as discreet and bounded entities. In the neoliberal context, services, including health care services, must be clearly defined, with clear expectations and boundaries: x is included, but y is not.

Mol focused on life with diabetes in order to say something more general about care – hence her choice to focus on logic, in order to explore care as an ideal type. At the same time, she avoided thinking of it as an ideal or universal good, or romanticizing it as some pre-modern quality – hence her choice of research topic and field site: "It means that this logic cannot be cast as a pre-modern 'care remnant' in an otherwise modern world. There is nothing nostalgic about diabetes care" (Mol, 2008, p. 10). In contrast with the logic of choice, the logic of care refers to a process rather than a clearly demarcated unit, product, or service. As described by Mol, care is not a transaction between professionals and patients but an ongoing, often messy process relying on experimentation and adjustments, on tinkering by all parties involved. In this sense, if we see patient choice as a way to involve patients in decision-making, this is not to say that the logic of care renders them passive. Yet, "[T]he logic of care is not preoccupied with our will, and with what we may opt for, but concentrates on what we do" (Mol, 2008, p. 7). This invitation to ponder the importance of willing, deciding, and taking charge is a potentially fruitful one in the context of a discussion about wellbeing. Choice in itself might not always be the best path to wellbeing. The choices available might not be appealing, or one can experience decision fatigue. Indeed, one might not be able to choose not to choose. This is not to say that people should not have a choice or make decisions, but this need not be understood as a lone individual making choices, walking down a path and deciding which road to take at junctures, navigating life's vicissitudes primarily relying on their own will.

How one's life unfolds is not merely a question of what one decides to do or what one chooses. A sense of agency, or a feeling that one can affect one's own path, that one is not merely thrown to the mercy of external forces, is often very important for one's sense of wellbeing (Renes & Aarts, 2018; Welzel & Inglehardt, 2010). A degree of agency seems desirable in terms of wellbeing but also carries a sense of responsibility that might be difficult to bear. If we take Mol's distinction between the logic of choice and the logic of care seriously, the *context* of choice emerges as fundamental.

In this sense, it may be helpful to think of agency and choice in the context of a life course. The metaphor of life as a journey, or a path, suggests that one travels alone and choices on this path figure as forks in the road. Yet life rarely presents us with clear junctures, and infrequently proceeds through orderly stages, at least not everywhere and for everyone. In some more institutionalized contexts, this may be the case, yet in places of crisis and uncertainty, life is less predictable. Against the background of uncertainty, Jennifer Johnson-Hanks (2002) has argued against the idea of life "stages," but her argument also touches upon the idea of life choices as such. These are often associated with particular life stages, presented as junctures at which the individual alone decides which path to take. Johnson-Hanks found that young Beti women often did not make choices or plans for the future, which was highly uncertain and in flux; instead, they exercised what she referred to as judicious opportunism.

Depending on the chances presented, one must exercise judgment about the next step to take. In my opinion, this idea can usefully be joined with the understanding of the context of relations of care. The situations that require navigation and judgment are constituted and framed by those in our circles of care. If we ask the following questions, a different way of looking at a life trajectory emerges: Whom do you care for? Who supported you, helped you? Who depends on you? Recognizing a deep dependency on others in many spheres of life (or even a lack of people who rely on us), presents our pursuit of wellbeing less in terms of will and choice, and more firmly in the context of relationships.

In other words, agency (and hence choice) is still important, but there is a need to rethink who the subject of choices and agentive navigation is. By attending to care, which encompasses groups and networks of people, we can see that decisions (and choice) are not taking place as discrete events, in isolation, made by lone individuals. Subjects of care encompass other people. By expanding the agentive locus, decentering the life course, and acknowledging that care always encompasses others, we do not render the subject of subjective wellbeing passive. We invite them to acknowledge the role of others in their lives, to recognize their dependencies and caring responsibilities. Attending to these relations can, in itself, be seen as therapeutic in some contexts (see also Kavedžija, 2020). Care, once again, brings people together.

"Care involves an act of reaching out, in a gesture that seeks to comfort, to connect, to heal – to make whole. To *integrate*" (Taylor, 2014, para. 1). Care is integrative. It creates social relationships and underlies social organization (see Thelen, 2015). It addresses human beings holistically, embodied human beings, not just some aspects of them. It brings various domains together (public, political, economic, private, intimate, bodily, and spiritual). The obstacles for care, the challenges it poses to wellbeing, can be located precisely when such integration is precluded or challenged, as Taylor (2014) powerfully recalled in her two stories of care. In the first, she recalled a medical trainee learning that she can guide people with dementia to hold a cup of water by gently cupping their hands around it when a muscle memory might kick in, and they might recall how to do it. She described the glint in the eye of the carer, when she tried it and it worked, the care worked! The other story is a more difficult one. In this one, a nurse recognizes her and recalls caring for her mother. When Taylor utters words of thanks, she goes on to say she is no longer working there, as she got fired. While looking after the urgent bodily needs of one older patient, another whom she was in charge of wandered outside (Taylor, 2014). Care reached its limit here. Attending to the integrative aspects of care and its limits of integration is a powerful way to evaluate and facilitate wellbeing, of both carers and the cared for.

Care also integrates the past, present, and future.

> In living with diabetes time is not a moment-by-moment affair. For while the past has left ineradicable traces within you, the future is already present too. You try to juggle with the future. The tight regulation in which you engage does not make you feel better now. Instead, you hope it will postpone the complications of your diabetes. It is good for later. The logic of care does not unfold in time. It folds time. (Mol, 2008, p. 54)

Some of the limits of care are also limits of time. When care works well, it enfolds people, spheres, and practices together in time; when time requires separation, the limits of care appear quickly.

3.7 Temporalities of Care

In order to care, the caregiver requires care and support, too. This does not mean that care is simply an exchange.[9] If seen as a relationship between two parties, it may appear asymmetrical, even if caregiving can be a source of meaning and fulfillment. Yet those who give care also require care, and this does not need to come only from the other party in a binary relationship. Indeed, it needs to come from other sources. The main thing that I learned from my older interlocutors in Japan, apart from the importance of cultivating the attitude of care, is the value of communities of care, in which care circulates and spreads. Furthermore, when considering care as effort, as labor, as work, it also becomes clear that good care takes time and yet is often urgent and pressing. The time of care might not accord with capitalist time reckoning.

Drawing on the influential work of Alfred Gell (1992), who suggested that humans do not merely measure or calculate time but rather navigate by using time maps (such as particular calendars or time-reckoning devices, which may vary culturally and historically), Laura Bear (2014) pointed to the simultaneous coexistence of multiple ways of understanding and navigating times, or multiple time maps. In other words, there might be several different time maps that one can look toward, such as the rhythm of the seasons, one's own biorhythm, a menstrual cycle, rising tides, a baby's nap schedule, or the time of

---

[9] "The reciprocity in caring relations is not contractual; that is, we do not expect the cared-for to balance the relation by doing what the one-caring (or carer) does" (Noddings, 2013, p. xxi).

a contemporary workplace, among others. While different time maps certainly can and often do clash, these tensions do not play out on an equal footing. Not all time maps carry equal influence in any given setting. No doubt, one's menstrual calendar does not carry much influence in most modern workplaces, nor does a young child's feeding or napping schedule matter very much to the city transportation timetables. The time maps of capitalist modernity (Bear, 2014) take precedence in many contexts, and thereby come into tension with the temporalities of care. These conflicts in time maps are inflected by power relations and have serious consequences for wellbeing.

Attending to temporalities of care makes clear that interventions and services addressing the wellbeing of an individual in isolation tend to fail to address the relations of care people are enmeshed in. When exploring temporalities of care, it becomes clear that if considering care as thriving in circulation, as enmeshed in a broad network of relationships, it is not possible to remedy insufficiencies merely by adding new forms of support and services. Even when these services correctly identify those in greatest need of support, merely offering them additional services (that come with additional time burden) may create further challenges rather than solutions. For example, it might be necessary to recognize that overburdened and overworked company employees' wellbeing is not merely their own. Hence, offering de-stress meditations and yoga classes to workers free of charge may seem like a nice intervention to bolster wellbeing, but probably does very little to address the underlying problem of an excessive workload or insufficient childcare or care leave. Clashes in time maps must be carefully assessed to understand the true context of wellbeing. When we attend to people as enmeshed in relations of care, a different vision of wellbeing comes to the fore.

3.8 Enfolding and Circulation of Care

Looking at the work of care, within the home and outside, in formal and informal settings, both unremunerated and monetized, it becomes clear that care requires us to shift our gaze away from the lone individual and toward their relations of care while further recognizing that these are enmeshed in wider networks and organizations. Care circulates broadly. Thus, it is easier to bring up children, educate young adults, work, provide the necessities for life, or support elders, from within networks of support. Care is integrative and works best when its various forms come together rather than clash. In some contexts – as I discussed in Section 1 – multigenerational living facilitates care for children and support for elders simultaneously, incorporating activities such as the communal preparation of foods and sustainable living.

Dyadic relations of care are often asymmetrical, and in complex ways. Returning to the example of older people in Chicago and their home carers, the asymmetry is present in two ways. Often, the older adults are more affluent, while their home carers are in a more financially precarious position. On the other hand, the elders rely on homeworkers for their support, including sensory mediation (Buch, 2013). Beyond and in addition to the complexities of racial and neoliberal inequalities, this example also reveals a deep asymmetry in many caring relationships. Yet, depending on the context, this asymmetry or unequal quality of caring relationships need not in itself be considered a bad thing, as it may be generative of broader social organizations (Thelen, 2015). The logic of care teaches us that there is a fundamental asymmetry in human relationships, one which does not bear calculation of simple give and take. This logic is fundamentally at odds with our sense of human personhood as fundamentally based on independence and equality. How can we be equal when one is so dependent on another? At the same time, care redefines ideas of exchange. Care may be based on a sense of obligation (and debt), but caregiving can simultaneously be deeply meaningful and rewarding. Care itself, while it can be embedded in financial exchange, resists such framing. If the logic of remuneration rests on paying off the labor in its entirety, this cannot be achieved; payment cannot easily erase a debt of gratitude to those who care. It is in this sense that the mathematics of productivity and efficiency does not do justice to care. Enmeshed in relations of care, we receive a lot, even while giving. Much of this plays out simultaneously. Care enfolds time, bringing people and activities closer together.

I would like to pause a little on this figure of folding. The most famous image of a fold is perhaps to be found in the work of Deleuze (1988), for whom it is akin to a fold in the fabric at the edge of a garment, say a trouser leg or a sleeve. The inner and outer layers of fabric meet here. Deleuze used this figure to think of a fundamental way in which persons internalize elements of the outside world. Here a *fold* is "the inside of thought" or a form of subjectivation in which the outer world is folded inward (Deleuze, 1988, p. 94). In another image, for example, in a recipe for a cake, we may be encouraged to fold the beaten egg whites, a wonderful soft foam, into the stodgy substance of the batter itself. Folding needs to be done with care to avoid damaging the fragile texture of the foam. Drawing on Deleuze's image, perhaps persons can be understood as foldings of care.

Folding has another dimension, a temporal one. It brings remote spheres closer together. Two points of the fabric, quite far apart, are brought close together in the fold. If modernity proceeds by segmenting reality into ever smaller units and spheres, seen as separate, this process tends to be clearly reflected in temporalities of capitalist modernity. Time to work is separate from the time to exercise, separate from the time to socialize, all playing out within rather rigidly demarcated boundaries (Giddens, 1991). Care, in contrast, beautifully and rather infuriatingly, stubbornly transgresses and frustrates those boundaries. Consider the (in)famous video clip of a foreign correspondent giving a comment on the current political situation, live on air, when his young child enters the room, resisting the boundaries between work and home. There are, no doubt, many reasons this was considered worthy of attention and even amusing, not least because such inter-domain overlaps and leakages are still remarkably rare and almost outrageous. The problem with such stubborn incursions of demands for care arises acutely when there is no *leeway*, no space to adapt, no slack to move and accommodate the urgent demand, for care has to be timely.

Care has a capacity to integrate and to enfold various spheres of activity – creative endeavors, food preparation, child minding, or care for plants, can often all be carried out alongside one another. Walking a dog is both care and exercise. Such a stroll might render a walk on a treadmill in the peculiar space of the gym and dedicated to keeping exercise separate from work, family, and even pets, less urgent or even unnecessary. Cycling to work embodies care for the environment, folding exercise back into the workday. This is not to romanticize these embedded relations of care but rather to call for a recognition of the centrality of relations of care in considerations of wellbeing, even in contexts where the proliferation of rigidly demarcated spheres of life risks obscuring lines of care. The path to recovery for those who wish to improve their wellbeing might well be to attend to their relations of care, to cultivate an attitude of care for others, for the very practice of care may attune us to the world positively. Shifting the discourse of wellbeing research away from subjective wellbeing, understood as centered and fundamentally seated within the person (figured as an individual), and toward a better understanding of relational configurations, might best be achieved through the study of relations of care.

4 Creativity

Anthropological research on creativity has consistently sought to enlarge our understanding of both what creativity means and how it plays out in social contexts, enfolded within a very broad range of practices. Creativity is seen as an ever-emerging, open-ended process, responsive and iterative. In this section, I argue that wellbeing hinges on creativity in fundamental ways, although the relationship is far from simple or straightforward. For a start, in and of itself, much like imagination (Sneath, Holbrad, & Pedersen, 2009), creativity is far from univocally positive. Conversely, much ingenuity can be found in acts of destruction. Undoubtedly, manipulation, seduction, and control can all be accompanied and made possible by creativity (Liep, 2001). The question thus becomes: what kind of creativity is most conducive to wellbeing, and why? In his seminal theory of ritual, Victor Turner (1979) described a particular stage found in many rituals, especially rites of passage, existing "betwixt and between" the more clearly delineated stages, which he described as *liminal*, as pertaining to the boundary, or to *limes* (in Latin). In the classic rites of passage such as initiation or coming-of-age ceremonies, the liminal stage is located between, say, childhood and adulthood. More broadly, liminality can be seen as a time of danger and uncertainty but also as a particularly fecund time of joy, play, and creativity. Times of uncertainty bear much resemblance to the experience of liminality, not least insofar as they bring with them a sense of potential and possibility. In what follows, I hope to show how it is creative attunement that transforms uncertainty into potential, in the process supporting wellbeing.

4.1 Cultural Creativity

Often when we tend to think of someone creative, our thoughts move to the creative genius of a lone individual, creating in relative isolation and producing innovative work in moments of inspiration. In anthropology and beyond, this way of thinking about creativity has been shown to be historically and culturally specific, originating in the Romantic era in Western Europe (Wilf, 2014). Moving away from such a focus on the individual, anthropological theories tend to focus on creativity as it relates to the processes of cultural reproduction and cultural change. John Liep (2001, p. 2) defined creativity as "activity that produces something new through the recombination and transformation of existing cultural practices or forms ... Creativity involves the acceptance of the novel in a social environment." Liep's definition introduces cultural forms into the definition of creativity but remains primarily focused on novelty and innovation. A preoccupation with creativity figured as innovation is arguably an effect of modernity. We should bear in mind that not all societies are equally interested in the production of novelty. Instead of being seen as a part of a timeless order of things, in modernity, "humanity finds itself in a condition where creation has moved into the present. The life trajectory of the individual and the course and shape of society are becoming a consciously human project" (Liep, 2001, p. 3). Hirsch and McDonald (2007), building on the work of the philosopher Charles Taylor, suggested that this understanding of creativity (as opposed to just something being seen as "creative") can be linked to the objectification of the imagination as a faculty which can be located somewhere in the mind or person, and can be studied in psychological terms: the locus of the production of novelty.

Linking creativity closely to innovation, as in Liep's account, excludes many forms of potentially creative activity and focuses on a relatively small proportion of achievements as being truly creative. His conceptualization acknowledges, nonetheless, some important social aspects in the context of recognition of the value or importance of the creative achievement. Ideas and things that are not recognized as worthwhile in a certain cultural context are not recognized as creative. If only certain relatively rare achievements are to be deemed creative, then true creativity is more likely to be attributed to a special category of people – those capable of such achievements – and moreover restricted to specific spheres.

Although Liep's understanding of creativity focuses on novelty and distinguishes more ordinary or mundane forms of creative practice from the "real" creativity of those who break with convention, other anthropological work seeks to move beyond the convention-innovation dichotomy. Tradition and cultural life both unfold in time, and life brings unpredictability – hence, no cultural script or blueprint offers a ready-made solution for every occasion, and application of these cultural forms always requires creative interpretation. As Rosaldo and his colleagues (1993) argued, "The healthy perpetuation of cultural traditions requires invention as well as rote repetition. Even decisions to alter nothing from the past will usually be thwarted because changing circumstances transform the meaning and consequences of dutifully repeated traditional actions" (p. 5). Viewed this way, creativity can be seen as located in a broad variety of cultural practices and not just those which explicitly result in innovation.

Two contrasting ways, then, of understanding creativity: a narrower conceptualization as (more or less radical) innovation; and a broader understanding as a cultural practice. These resonate in turn with two different points of departure in understanding human societies. The first point of departure is a model of stasis and stability, which requires that change be explained and justified. The other is processual and emphasizes change, whereas stability requires explanation, given that "everything that happens is new unrepeatable and not wholly predictable from what went before" (Barber, 2007, p. 25). In recent years, the latter, more processual approach has won favor in anthropological circles, and creativity is commonly seen as a widespread cultural practice that unfolds in numerous spheres of life.[10]

---

[10] "From this perspective, mundane everyday activities become as much the locus of cultural creativity, as the arduous ruminations of the lone artist or scientist" (Rosaldo, Lavie, & Narayan, 1993, p. 5).

4.2 Imitation and Innovation

"Creation is a bending of form to one's will, not the manufacture of form ex nihilo"
(Sapir, 1924, p. 414, cited in Rosaldo, Lavie, & Narayan, 1993, p. 5).

Rather than conceiving of novelty as a radical break with the past, with convention or tradition, the creative act should be seen as emerging from culturally available possibilities. Instead of being a creation *ex nihilo*, creative work brings elements, influences and insights from a range of available resources in a process of recombination and selection (Rosaldo, Lavie, & Narayan, 1993). Reflection upon the close links between imitation and creativity is not new, of course, and can be traced to (among others) the French sociologist Gabriel Tarde, who argued that in each instance of imitation something new might arise; every imitation has the potential for innovation (Barry & Thrift, 2007). Much apparently spontaneous and innovative work relies on a long process of socialization and practice, imitating and inhabiting the boundaries of genre and convention (Wilf, 2014). For example, calligraphers in Japan dedicate much time to the practice of copying (*rinsho*) the works of classic calligraphy. The cultural status of these copies is high, and they are often displayed in their own right. Nakamura (2007, p. 80) argued that "what is valued is a different kind of creativity, one that does not oppose the original to the imitation but rather has imitation at its very source." The practice of copying, or reproduction, focuses at first on the configuration and shape of the characters but later emphasizes the spirit of the calligraphic work, moving finally to reproduction from memory, allowing more space for an interpretation of the work. The practice leads to an embodied knowledge, which the practitioner is later supposed to move away from, in order to develop their own style (Nakamura, 2007). In this account, creativity emerges from practice and copying rather than appearing in a radical break from the past. Embodied skill animates the movements, informing the move toward the new.

For example, students in a US jazz college described by Wilf (2012) immerse themselves in musical performances which they imitate and learn to inhabit. This example is interesting not only because it comes from the United States rather than one of the cultural contexts more commonly associated with rote learning and tradition but also because jazz as a genre is closely associated with improvisation. Learning to immerse oneself in music requires one to play and improvise alongside skilled and experienced musicians. As opportunities to do this in live performances diminished, college instructors increasingly relied on musical recordings: "[B]y means of rule-governed appropriation of such technologies, students manage not only to 'be on stage' with a past jazz master such as Coltrane but also to fuse with him, in this way 'ritually inhabiting' the creativity of the master" (Wilf, 2012, pp. 35–37). Examples such as these imply that innovation and imitation do not stand in tension but embrace one another.

4.3 In a Subjunctive Mood: Liminality and Creativity

"Since liminal time is not controlled by the clock it is a time of enchantment when anything might, even should, happen"

(Turner, 1979, p. 465).

Although creativity can readily be found in the mundane and the everyday, certain moments or situations are especially fecund and full of potential. Liminality is a particularly apt term for understanding these uncertain transition times. As I noted before, liminal refers to a boundary between states, particularly in the context of rites of passage such as initiation rites, weddings, or funerals, in which participants transition from one life status to another. Building on the work of folklorist van Gennep, Victor Turner (1970) explored liminality in the rites of passage found in all societies (though they hold particular importance in many smaller-scale societies), which have three distinct stages: separation (from the earlier status, group or state), margin (or limes), and aggregation. Liminal persons are seen as belonging neither to their earlier stage nor to the new stage they are moving toward, and, as such, they are seen to be "betwixt and between," bound by neither set of rules, and dangerous, powerful, and polluting (Turner, 1970, p. 97).

In discussing the structural aspect of liminality, I mentioned how neophytes are withdrawn from their structural positions and consequently from the values, norms, sentiments, and techniques associated with those positions. They are also divested of their previous habits of thought, feeling, and action. During the liminal period, neophytes are alternately forced and encouraged to think about their society, their cosmos, and the powers that generate and sustain them. Liminality may be partly described as a stage of reflection. (Turner, 1970, p. 105)

Turner outlined the characteristics of the liminal as reflexive and potentially dangerous, but also full of potential. He ended his study by inviting researchers to attend to ritual (and other) processes as they unfold, as much is to be learned from the interim stages, not by merely attending to the stages at the beginning and end. This is an invitation that scholars of creativity should take seriously, still today, for it is all too easy to focus on creative outputs and neglect the process itself.

We are now in a position to consider how creativity relates to wellbeing. It is interesting to note that the liminal is always between two stages or statuses, one which precedes it and another which follows. It is distinct from these statuses, and removed from them. As such, liminal experiences cannot be classified into the usual categories, which is why they are so often seen as dangerous and problematic. This mid-transition experience may be uncomfortable and unsettling but provides an opportunity for reflection. In his later work, Turner sought to explore liminal experiences beyond ritual, including work, leisure, play, and art. Unlike rituals in small-scale societies, which tend to encompass everyone and which are often compelling and compulsory, in industrial societies, the liminal sphere emerges among smaller groups. In these groups, there is a degree of voluntary engagement (as it is not compulsory like the rituals described earlier) and a removal from the mainstream, but a similar sense of *communitas* (see Turner, 1977, p. 47). Rather than liminal, Turner refers to the latter as "liminoid." While in the liminal stage of the ritual much is reversed – power structures, roles, expectations – liminoid can be seen as subversive in its departure from the mainstream. Communitas is here defined as "social anti-structure," and stands in opposition to static structures in societies, or to organizations and rules. Instead, communitas encompasses play and collective "unmediated communication, or even communion" (Turner, 1977, p. 46).

Turner pointed to a link between communitas and the experiences of "flow" which, as famously described by the psychologist Csikszentmihalyi, rely on intense focus (on a limited stimulus) which leads to a merging of action and awareness. In other words, one's self is immersed in the activity, and in control of the process. This in turn increases a feeling of confidence. Turner considered communitas to be a form of shared flow, which involves "an ego-less state that is its own reward" (Turner, 1979, p. 488). This reference to the intrinsic nature of rewards in the state of flow, or what Csikszentmihalyi called autotelic activity, which has no outside aim but the process itself, is of particular relevance for an understanding of creativity and wellbeing. In his discussion of the challenges of midlife (mid-part of adulthood), Kiran Setiya (2017) took from Aristotle a helpful distinction between telic and atelic activities; the former are oriented toward an aim or achievement. The latter do not appear to have a clearly defined, external purpose, and thus resemble the autotelic character of flow. Atelic activities cannot simply be completed, for they are not oriented toward a final state (Deng, 2018). According to Setiya, a midlife crisis is more likely to ensue when one engages predominantly in telic activities (buying a house, say, finding a partner, or finishing a book manuscript). Once attained, those goals disappear, and with them, the sense of purpose they created, leaving behind a void. Of course, many activities could be framed equally in either terms. For example, one could train to complete a marathon, or use a marathon competition as a milestone in an ongoing training process; I could write to finish a book manuscript, or because writing allows me to order my thoughts. Setiya's suggestion to focus on atelic activities has been understood by some as a form of presentism, a type of temporal ontology that favors the present moment (Deng, 2018). In contrast, we can contend (with Csikszentmihalyi) that creative process can be seen as an aim in itself, in a way that is not temporally fixed. I shall develop this point in the following section, in the context of navigation.

Turner (1977) examined the relationship of flow to liminality, situating the liminoid in work, play, and leisure, but showed that flow moves across the work and leisure divide. In this sense, creativity integrates spheres that became separated in contemporary (post-) industrial societies. Turner also drew attention to the embodied qualities of flow, linking it to flow in a broader sense: touch and foreplay, for instance, precipitate bodily flow in lactation and sexual intercourse. Flow experienced in group activity (be it ritual or other type of communitas), too, has an embodied and visceral, often exhilarating or almost erotic quality, and could be seen as an immersive, all-encompassing experience. It is in these kinds of moments, in rituals, sporting events, or art performances, that the boundaries of self-appear to dissolve.

Considering the conditions of marginality and uncertainty in terms of liminality has its benefits. The liminoid sphere reframes that which would otherwise be merely transitional or marginal, by highlighting its capacity for immediacy and immersion, as well as providing a reflection on the status quo. Turner (1979) linked liminal temporality to potential, to a sense that anything might happen, like the subjunctive mood. In this sense, the liminal and the liminoid offer a space of potential. This is not to say that creativity does not happen in ordinary ways. After all, even artists have resisted the construction of art as a sphere apart (Sansi, 2014). Nonetheless, attending to the way creativity is fuelled by the liminal allows us to characterize creativity as processual, in temporal terms, while at the same time framing the uncertain nature of the liminal moment in terms of potential. The capacity of the creative process to reframe temporality is relevant for an exploration of the links between creativity and wellbeing. In what follows, I attend to the temporal and processual aspects of creativity as a form of collaboration.

4.4 Improvisation and Creativity: The Collaborative Process

In his classic work *The Savage Mind*, Claude Lévi-Strauss (1962) drew a now-infamous comparison between so-called mythical (or wild) and scientific thought. While stressing that both modes of thought are rational, he drew attention to some important differences. These are perhaps best captured by a metaphorical distinction between a *bricoleur* (a handyman of sorts) and an engineer. The engineer works from a blueprint to change the world around them, creating specialized tools for the task ahead. The bricoleur, by contrast, is apt at numerous diverse tasks and works with materials and tools that are already available, at his disposal, and adapts the project to what he already has. Rather than working to a blueprint, the bricoleur improvises:

> Consider him at work and excited by his project. His first practical step is retrospective. He has to turn back to an already existent set made up of tools and materials, to consider or reconsider what it contains and, finally and above all, to engage in a sort of dialogue with it. (Lévi-Strauss, 1962, p. 12)

Two things stand out in this quote, in the context of a discussion of creativity and wellbeing. First, Lévi-Strauss draws attention to the propensity of the bricoleur (and, by extension, mythical thought) to proceed by working from what is available, by refashioning what is there. In this process of refashioning and using existing tools and materials, a certain likeness is drawn out, when a new element is placed in an existing arrangement or structure. This mode of thought is analogical – it functions through likeness or analogy. For Lévi-Strauss, myth is a tool that is used to address a problem (rather than resolve it outright, as scientific thought might attempt); to tackle it in a similar way to art or poetry, namely through metaphor and likeness. "The principal virtue of myths is to transpose one problem into the terms of a formally similar one, belonging to another domain, an operation that they endlessly repeat, to the point of 'exhaustion', as they follow their 'spiral' development" (Wiesman, 2007, p. 41). Myths, like art, offer a model of the world that reduces it through likeness, by seeking out analogous instances, thus rendering the world more manageable. Second, the bricoleur moves her thought and work along by engaging in a dialogue with his tools and materials. His work is a kind of recombination of elements within a symbolic system, but a creative engagement nonetheless.

This aspect of attention to and engagement with materials resonates with some contemporary anthropological discussions of creativity. For example, Ingold and Hallam (2007) focused on improvisation, rather than innovation, precisely to challenge the dichotomy between novel and traditional, or continuity and change, that underpins so many earlier discussions of creativity. This modernist distinction is not particularly fruitful, as people are always required to improvise as they move through lives in changing circumstances. No cultural script encompasses all the factors and eventualities. Yet, the key difference between creativity as innovation and creativity as improvisation is not their relationship to convention or tradition (insofar as the former steps outside it while the latter remains bound by it). For Ingold and Hallam (2007), the key difference lies in the temporal focus; the former attends to outcomes and the products of creativity, and the latter attends to the process itself. In their analysis of improvisation, they seek to capture the ongoing nature of the creative process, alongside active engagement with materials.

Understanding creativity as a forward orientation highlights its temporal dimension: the creative process itself unfolds in time. The surrounding world is changing too, as time is passing.

> This process is going on, all the time, in the circulations and fluxes of the materials that surround us and indeed of which we are made – of the earth we stand on, the water that allows it to bear fruit, the air we breathe, and so on. These materials are life-giving, and their movements, mixtures and bindings are creative in themselves. (Hallam & Ingold, 2007, p. 11).

Making and growing are more alike than they might seem at first glance. As Ingold and Hallam (2014, p. 6) noted, "similar processes would generate similar results." These processes, of course, unfold in time. The creative process, as well as any output or product, is itself always emergent (see Kavedžija, 2021). This means that steps in the creative processes are not predetermined by a total and coherent vision of a creative output at the end, a mental blueprint of sorts. At every stage the unpredictable elements may enter the process and the steps might need to be adapted and adjusted. This temporal quality of movement can be linked with unpredictability and uncertainty – the metaphor of navigation is helpful here as a way of capturing this, as in navigating an uncertain terrain. Navigation is a term that originated in a maritime context, but in fact the undulating, ever shifting surface of the sea highlights an important feature of navigation through the social world as it shifts and unfolds around one – hence Vigh's (2009) description of social navigation as "motion squared." As social actors move through the world, they interact with others, with their environment and the social forces around them, but do not remain unchanged. Practice is a form of interaction; hence, the actors change the context as they move through it, but, in addition, change also occurs from many other directions.

The creative process, similarly, unfolds in time, at its own pace, but also affected and framed by multiple temporalities. First, it can be framed by the immediate temporality of the event (Kavedžija, 2021). These could quite literally be art events, such as exhibitions or performances, of which the creative work is a part – where they originate as an inspiration, say, or as a collaboration. To the extent that work can be created with a particular art event in mind (in the future), the temporality of the event resembles the temporality of a project (Sansi, 2014), most often associated with having an end point, a deadline before which a body of work must be prepared or completed. Furthermore, the temporality of the artists' daily life, mundane rhythms of life and living with others, responsibilities and family obligations, other work, routines, and artist's own life course frame the work further. This is true whether the artist is young or old, advanced in career or burgeoning. All of these circumstances offer important framings for the creative process. Creative temporality thus itself floats (or, we might say, struggles against the current) of various temporal flows, in a kind of complex navigation. Due to its interactive, iterative, dialogical, and open-ended qualities of multiple engagements, the creative process is itself uncertain. Its outcome is never guaranteed, or entirely known.

4.5 Work and Creativity

"Love of labour is a contradiction in terms"

(Bentham, 1983, p. 104).

How to understand the statement in the epigraph? When equated with toil or effort, labor is easily construed in opposition to wellbeing and fulfillment. This kind of conceptualization of labor also places it in opposition to leisure. Yet according to Skidelski and Skidelski (2012), this is an overly narrow and negative perspective on work, which further does a disservice to the understanding of leisure. True leisure, they argue (with Kant), is an activity without a purpose (or, rather, an extrinsic purpose or end):[11]

> [Leisure is] "purposiveness without purpose," as Kant put it. The sculptor engrossed in cutting marble, the teacher intent on imparting a difficult idea, the musician struggling with a score, a scientist exploring the mysteries of space and time – such people have no other aim than do what they are doing well. They may receive an income for their efforts, but that income is not what motivates them. In our terms, they are engaged in leisure, not toil (Skidelski & Skidelski, 2012, p. 9).

In other words, leisure should not be equated simply with rest or passivity. Instead, it is best understood in opposition to toil, labor with an extrinsic motivation (such as remuneration). In this sense, activities that are not motivated by necessity, are more spontaneous, or experienced as inherently interesting, valuable, or engrossing, are less like toil and more akin to leisure. Many forms of meaningful work could fit this description.

It has recently been argued that although work has become an increasingly important yardstick of a person's value, as many as 40 percent of people living in contemporary Western contexts do not consider their work to be socially or personally meaningful (Graeber, 2018). As such, it is crucial to understand the circumstances of those who are unable or unwilling to participate fully in the world of work, or who avoid or reject this dominant life model, as well as

---

[11] Good care is also seen as being without a purpose beyond the practice of care itself, as explored in the previous section.

the ways in which work may come to be constructed and experienced as meaningful.[12] This brings us to one particularly widely discussed model of meaningful work: craftsmanship.

4.6 Craftsmanship as a Model of Meaningful Work

> The laborer with a sense of craft becomes engaged in the work in and for itself; the satisfactions of working are their own reward; the details of daily labor are connected in the worker's mind to the end product; the worker can control his or her own actions at work; skill develops within the work process; work is connected to the freedom to experiment . . .
>
> (Wright Mills, 1951, pp. 220–223)

If craft has received considerable attention as a model for meaningful work, this is no doubt in part because it figures as a necessary counterpoint to labor in industrial contexts, in which the worker is seen as having considerably less autonomy and control over the production process, not to mention the means of production. In other words, craft is interesting as the quintessential form of non-alienated labor. It is also a prime example of what Ingold (2013, p. xi) called "thinking through making." For philosopher Richard Sennett, a focus on craft is as a technique for a particular way of life, one in which thinking and making are intimately entwined. Sennett (2008) argued against an understanding of crafts-manship as a way of life that has receded with the advent of industrial produc-tion. In his view, it captures the widespread desire to do one's work well, for the inherent satisfaction it affords.

Not unlike Ingold, Sennett (2008) is interested in exploring ways of knowing, particularly as they play out in the relationship between the hand and the head. Sennett's aim is to rescue the image of the worker-maker from its association with unfreedom, developed most notably in Hannah Arendt's (1958) seminal work *The Human Condition*. Arendt distinguished the necessity of work of the *animal laborans*, the worker who is pressed by need, from the constrained yet productive *homo faber*, a human as a maker; and from the freedom of thought and expression as embodied by human as *zoon politikon*, a creature of discourse and innovation. Sennett aimed instead to show how thought underpins much of the productive effort, how no process of making is divorced from thinking, suggesting that for Arendt, the mind engages once labor is done.[13] Another,

---

[12] As creativity is increasingly recognized as an indispensable part of a wide variety of professions, the idea of creativity gains prominence while at the same time growing even more diluted and vague. Discourses of creativity have become ever more a part of the postindustrial workplace and co-opted in managerial practice, which arguably further redefines being creative as implying being self-driven, or an independent problem-solver, or simply resourceful (Sansi, 2015).

[13] See also Dewey (1980/1934) for a similar argument against setting art apart from practical endeavors.

more balanced view is that thinking and feeling are contained within the process of making (Sennett, 2008). Trevor Marchand, an anthropologist who apprenticed as a craftsman, similarly argued that craft practice is a form of problem-solving, and that problem-solving takes place at all stages of the process. This includes planning, selecting one's materials and tools (and even fashioning or adapting them, if necessary), and working within a set of financial and temporal constraints. "In sum, craftwork provides an ideal setting for witnessing the emergence of a vast diversity of challenges and, more importantly, for observing our human creative potential for overcoming them" (Marchand, 2017, p. 2). Meaningful work, then, is a way of knowing and thinking in an embodied way that involves problem-solving, and in which creative spaces open up. Challenges and problems are opportunities for creative problem-solving, if one is given enough decision-making autonomy.

Craftsmanship is skilled work, and requires practice and dedication. The honing of skill, or processes of enskilment, are at the heart of much anthropological writing on creativity and making, such as Gowlland's (2019) exploration of the sociality of enskilment in a pottery workshop in China. Enskilment emerges here clearly as a social process, and while people acquire skills by practicing them alone, much of what they learn is with and from others. The learning of skills takes place in "enchronic time" (Enfield, 2009), built around the idea that certain interactions and communications, including gestures, do not merely follow one another, but are linked to each other in a causal manner. Enchronic time in the context of learning a craft unfolds in clusters or parallel sequences, rather than a uniform homogenous sequence (Gowlland, 2019). Some actions need to be performed simultaneously, as Gowlland described with reference to the example of being taught by a master potter in China. The master instructs the anthropologist apprentice not only to place the tools on the pot swiftly at the same time, but also to listen to the sound they should be making, in a process of education of attention. The sociality of the skill remains within the person of the maker, long after the teaching event has ended. Even if the practice of craft is sometimes a solitary endeavor, the skill, often developed and transmitted in a distinctly social way, continues to inform the creative process.

What then is the relationship of craft-like work to wellbeing? As noted, craft is sometimes used as a shorthand for work well done and for its own sake (Sennett, 2008). That is, it is work with its own inherent pleasures and intrinsic motivation. It can be associated with intense attention and a sense of motivation, mastery, and control. The requisite skills are learned, often through some form of apprenticeship, and it is in that sense social and often traditional, yet requires attentive adaptability and creative responsiveness. This sense of openness to others and adaptability are seen as a powerful counterbalance to alienated labor.

Biao Xiang (Qianni & Shifan, 2020) discussed the spirit of craftsmanship as an antidote to "involution," or the trap of increasingly higher stakes to maintain the status quo. It is an arms race to preserve social status that many contemporary industrialized societies appear to be facing. In recent years, the concept of involution has captured the public imagination in China as a way of describing a particularly acute downside of "progress" that comes with increasing affluence in Chinese cities. It affects many who are trying to secure a way of life that involves a steady job, a car, and a house. To stand a chance in this competitive environment, where a race for jobs is ever fiercer, education becomes increasingly more onerous. Child-rearing requires ever more dedication, and involves a variety of after-school activities or tutoring. According to Xiang, the term "involution" originally referred to the laborious, high-stakes maintenance of the status quo in contexts such as agriculture, where in order to expand agricultural gains, a greater workforce was required, but all the gains were consumed by the increase in the workforce. The meaning of the term has now shifted, however, from a high-stakes equilibrium trap to a spiral trap in which ever-higher stakes are involved. Xiang linked this with homogenous goals and expectations: most people in Chinese society have similar goals, and therefore have to compete fiercely for them. Comparing China with Japan, Xiang suggested that one antidote to involution might be the spirit of craftsmanship, focusing on a task and excelling at it. He offered by way of example the specialist attention given by a chef in a restaurant who specializes in a particular genre of cooking, only serving a few select dishes, and paying extreme attention to the ingredients and their provenance. In doing so, such a craftsman invokes the work and involvement of all those who helped to make the materials or ingredients she works with. In this sense, we could argue (with Xiang) that an antidote to involution, as a particularly acute version of the hedonic treadmill, would consist in a different way to define goals, by focusing on involvement of others and attention to the mastery of the task at hand.[14]

4.7 In Praise of Leeway: Temporality of Creativity

Mr Okano was already sitting at the window table of a small neighborhood café when I arrived, even though I was a little early myself. His dark-rimmed glasses glimmered in the bright light of the summer morning. Mr Okano had recently retired but continued to work three days a week, and agreed to talk to me about his work in a pharmaceutical laboratory. His retirement meant a reduced income and

---

[14] "Hedonic treadmill" refers to the influence of positive and negative events on happiness levels experienced by individuals. According to this framework people adapt relatively quickly to changing circumstances and return to a level of happiness that is akin to their set point. Recent studies have suggested that hedonic treadmill theories of adaptation require some revision, including accounting of the findings that some people's hedonic set point changes over time (Diener, Lucas, & Scollon, 2009).

some loss of prestige, but also opened up a little more space for reading and thinking. Before, when working long hours, he "simply had no leeway," he told me. Now, he finally had the time to engage his research interests with a renewed vigor.[15]

Mr. Okano was not the only person I met in Japan who complained that long working hours made it hard to work productively. Many also mentioned a lack of financial leeway, or family leeway, or simply lack of time, as challenges to working well and feeling well. Leeway is often understood as a margin of freedom to act, a degree of flexibility to make decisions or think. It can refer to a variety of circumstances, including time, space, money, or emotional capacity. I find that this concept is particularly interesting when it comes to wellbeing. With material resources and security this is most obvious, as it is well known that income or material possessions only have an impact on people's subjective wellbeing up to a certain point, and once this threshold is reached, they do not have much impact on how people feel. What if what is needed is just enough to have a feeling of a certain degree of safety and flexibility, some leeway? Similarly, I think it is helpful for thinking about other resources, such as time.

I was reminded of this idea of leeway when I was discussing work and wellbeing in a culture and wellbeing seminar with my students, as we talked about workplace values in the United Kingdom. Creativity, productivity, and efficiency were mentioned by my students as among the most important values; yet these can sometimes be in tension. When efficiency and productivity are emphasized, leeway is viewed as "slack." It is seen as something to be eliminated – simply unused time, or an imposed excessive cost. This often makes sense, but can also lead to situations that reduce leeway so much that no space for creative exploration, accidental encounters, or spontaneous thinking remains. Sometimes, productivity and efficiency are heralded as a way to save on costs, but as mental health and other problems ensue when the temporalities of workplace and care collide (see Section 2), or as the pace of work increases to the point of a crisis of creativity (where people struggle to come up with solutions and ideas), the palliative measures introduced to restore creativity, such as yoga or mindfulness sessions for employees, for instance, only go as far as to redress the balance. Productivity conceptualized as efficiency, in other words, may get in the way of leeway, which is crucial for both creativity and wellbeing. At the same time, there is an imperative to be creative, as argued by Hirsch and McDonald (2007), who call this attitude the cult of creativity.

---

[15] I met Mr. Okano in 2019, during my research on work and wellbeing in Japan, funded by Japan Foundation.

The importance of having room to create, to think and have ideas, featured strongly in many of my conversations and interviews with Japanese artists (see also Kavedžija, 2019), in my research on art as work.[16] One of my interlocutors, explaining why she decided to leave secure employment in a photography studio, mentioned her need to remove herself from a busy environment filled with everyday conversations and to create a quiet space for herself. Another said she left a well-paid job in a graphic design studio because the images filled up her imagination and affected her way of working, leaving too little space for her own creative work. A third person explained why she left a white-collar job even though the hours were not especially long: there was too much happening, she felt too busy, and there were too many stimuli. All this meant there was no leeway for their creative endeavors.

This feeling of there being "too many stimuli," of too much happening, highlights the limits of attention. This can be linked to contemporary phenomenological discussions of attention that highlight its embodied qualities. In her analysis of depressive states, Lucy Osler (2021) developed the useful idea of bodily saturation. In contrast to descriptions of depression as a sense of emptiness, Osler pointed to this sense being a feeling that nonetheless occupies the person experiencing it, not unlike a strong stimulus such as pain (or orgasm), which takes over the emotional field, causing other experiences to recede or slip away. Bodily saturation refers to this feeling of being overwhelmed, or taken over by a sensation, at capacity. This capacity is not fixed and it can change over time.[17]

The creative process requires leeway to avoid a feeling of being overwhelmed, to preserve some room and avoid saturation; or on the contrary – to create such space as to allow for complete saturation, as one might hope for in experiencing art, hoping to be awash in the sensation. Bodily saturation might be useful for an analysis of the relation between creativity and wellbeing to the extent it emphasizes the critical importance of leeway for both, while also pointing to the possibility of cultivating an expanded affective capacity. Attending to the cultivation of various affective capacities is particularly useful. Increased capacity in this sense can be imagined as better capacity for flow. Instead of thinking of it as the capacity of a container, affective capacity can be thought of as a flow capacity, the capacity to convey. Being capacious need not imply the ability to hold, absorb, or take in more (stimuli, burden, toil), but

---

[16] This research project was conducted in 2013 and funded by JSPS and supported by Osaka University.

[17] Responding to a critique that vessel-like metaphors for organisms have serious limitations as the limits of affectivity are not fixed (Leonelli, 2021), Osler also pointed out that the capacity is not the same for different people, or even the same people at different times.

rather, as a connective feature, can indicate how much one can transmit. Creative process is, in this sense, a skill that informs how one passes affect on to others and modulates this transmission deliberately. This, I believe, is exemplified in the practices and arts of living well that constitute the skills of conviviality, as discussed in Section 1.

4.8 Process and Movement

In the exhibition, the bottles of various shapes and sizes are lined up on a long wooden plank. The glass ranges in hue from transparent to blue and blue-green, but very pale. All the bottles reflect the light, as if they were made from mirrors. The inside of them appears to be coated with a silvery substance. This artwork, entitled *Silvering (parallel water)* was made by Ai Kawano. In a recent Open Studio Conversation on the topic of working with hands (handicraft) and magic, Kawano- san showed photographs of this work. The process was discovered when old glass was found in archaeological findings, when it occurred naturally. Mineral substances in the soil reacted and created the metallic coating. She now uses chemicals to recreate this process. Which one is more magic? There is a sense of extraordinary about this beautiful effect coming into being naturally, in the ground, but it feels magic to replicate quickly something that naturally takes place over a long period of time.

The artwork described in the earlier excerpt from my field notes appears to engage in a form of "time tricking," or "practices that manipulate, coordinate, structure or reorder knowledge about temporal processes" (Ringel, 2016, p. 25). Time tricking has also been described as "many different ways in which people individually and collectively attempt to modify, manage, bend, distort, speed up, slow down or structure the times they are living in" (Moroşanu & Ringel, 2016, p. 1). While the artwork described earlier deliberately plays with temporality, the work involved in the creative processes in general, by interfering with materials, object, or atmospheres, affects the temporality experienced. Creative work is, without doubt, a form of temporal agency. Furthermore, the creative process, being always open ended and uncertain, harnesses the open-ended quality of the everyday. In this sense, creative practice encapsulates the liminoid qualities discussed earlier: of danger, uncertainty, and potential, thereby reframing the creative experience as one in which attending to the unexpected, and even collaborating with it, is itself expected, and perhaps even welcomed.

Creative practice can thus be seen as a form of attunement that is of particular importance for wellbeing. By orienting attention to the processes of collaboration and improvisation, it transforms uncertainty and danger into resources. Creative attunement orients practitioners toward time as potentiality – a different type of resource. As creative engagements are open to improvisation, responsive, and open ended, this type of attention not only fosters focus and a sense of control (as claimed by psychologists), it also refashions material and temporal resources. Because creative engagement is, in principle, open to the influences and effects of various materials, media, and other collaborators, it can be seen as a way of educating the attention. It attunes us to others, and to temporal uncertainty, in a positive and open way.

5 Conclusion: Wellbeing as a Process

What can we learn about wellbeing when we attend to conviviality, care, and creativity? One thing these have in common is that they are all processual. This is not simply an essay about happiness in the community, the family, or work as *components* of wellbeing. By shifting the focus away from stable entities and structures and instead emphasizing processes and practices of conviviality, care, and creativity, it offers a different perspective on wellbeing, one that is itself processual and relational. To say that wellbeing is relational is not merely to state that relationships are important. It is necessary to shift the focus away from individuals, and to conceive of persons as continuously constituted through interactions and their caring relationships with others. Wellbeing is never an achievement, in other words; it is not something to be attained or possessed. It is, rather, a quality of how the multiple relationships that constitute our lives unfold over time.

Taking the social and relational qualities of wellbeing seriously demands careful attention to the nature of the subject in subjective wellbeing. Rather than departing from individual subjects, I have argued that we must attend to persons as constituted through their relations of care. Fostering wellbeing, too, requires attention to the networks of care which might be in need of support or repair. In order to scaffold wellbeing effectively, it is essential to create the conditions for these caring relations to function. Saying that wellbeing is social invites us to think of wellbeing as playing out in social situations and interactions, which is to say convivially; but also as a way of highlighting that the skills and practices required to live well are themselves social. They are socially constructed, transmitted, and socialized.

5.1 Of Flow and Flux: Navigating Wellbeing

To think of wellbeing as processual requires an acknowledgment that it unfolds in a changing environment. We not only move through life with others, but do so on shifting terrain. Moving through life is less like walking a well-trodden path on stable ground, and more like navigating a boat on undulating waters (Vigh, 2009). Creative processes, as the previous section showed, unfold in complex, collaborative interactions between persons, materials, and an environment that is itself constantly changing – which makes improvisation necessary. This brings with it a degree of uncertainty, which should not, however, be seen merely as a challenge or nuisance. As discussions of liminality show, uncertainty (and even the danger associated with it) can be productive and fecund. If creativity involves navigation and improvisation, it is also open to the effects of others – to ideas and influences from other people, to the qualities of materials, and so on. In this sense, creative navigation requires open, productive, and careful attention to the world around us. How we move through life depends on others, too. Our encounters and interactions, as well as our relationships with others, can open new possibilities, and support us on our way. But they also make other options less viable. In this sense, life choices, too, are enmeshed in networks of care.

Considering wellbeing as processual and relational, and hence as a form of social navigation, brings us to questions of agency and control and their consequences for wellbeing. On the one hand, it is clear that recognizing our entanglements with others – as we strive to live well together, share convivial skills, depend on one another, and share creative endeavors, in interactions with other entities and species – all place some limitations on individual agency. But if we conceive of persons as constituted through these relations of care, as temporary and ongoing folds of caring relationships, then the recognition that we depend on others is less a restriction of agency than the very phenomenon on which agency depends. This is exemplified by the attitude fostered by those who engage in various forms of processual creative work, where the input from the materials or other collaborators is seen as much a productive contribution as a delimitation. Cultivating an exploratory, open attitude of creativity that focuses on the process itself, and not the output alone, transforms uncertainty (which might otherwise be conceptualized as danger or risk) into a resource. The open-ended nature of the process might open us up to productive engagements with others.

The processual nature of wellbeing also orients us to questions of time and temporality. In this essay, I have argued for the importance of leeway for living well. Leeway resists the logic of efficiency that reconfigures it as slack or merely inefficient use of extra time (or resources, including human resources). This is particularly noticeable in relation to creative processes, which require space and time. Furthermore, time is important for enskillment and the cultivation of practices important for creativity, but also for conviviality. In order to live well together we need to master the convivial arts. Similarly, exploring temporalities of care points to the strain that conflicting temporalities can exert over those who are involved in care, even while care can bring previously separate domains together.

5.2 Affective Ecologies of Health

Alongside increasing inequality and environmental collapse, mental health is one of the great challenges facing contemporary societies. Anthropological research indicates some of the ways in which these issues are deeply intertwined; this too calls for an understanding of wellbeing as fundamentally relational. One way to think of wellbeing as encompassing more than one person is to consider it in terms of affect. Such affects can be seen to pervade not just people or communities but also spaces and environments. Yael Navaro-Yashin (2012) depicted landscapes of ruination left behind as the Greek-Cypriots migrated or perished following the outbreak of violence with Turkish-Cypriots in the 1970s. Navaro-Yashin related the melancholy feelings experienced by Turkish Cypriots with the environment they live in, particularly the looted land, through the metaphor of ruination, which she proposed refers to "the material remains or artefacts of destruction and violation, but also to the subjectivities and residual affects that linger, like a hangover, in the aftermath of violence" (2012, p. 162). Fields are left unattended, property in ruin, out of fear that the earlier inhabitants might return.

In a sense, humans and our nonhuman companions now inhabit a global landscape of ruination, threat, and injustice. Pervasive environmental destruction, violence, and inequality are impossible to ignore. Various forms of disquiet are ever present in the world around us. Any theory of wellbeing that does not take into account our intimate interconnection with nonhuman as well as human others is therefore painfully incomplete.[18] A different attitude is required not only toward other living beings but also toward those entities we tend to understand as objects, materials, or technologies. In his discussion of tools for conviviality, Ivan Illich (1973) argued against a narrow understanding of industrial productivity as a principle of social organization that reduced people to the status of consumers. Instead, Illich proposed a free use of tools to foster conviviality and collaboration, henceforth restricted by institutional arrangements. An obsession with productivity can curb free and creative interactions between people. If we are to foster conviviality, therefore, we must also approach tools and technologies in a way that facilitates sharing and creative collaboration.

5.3 Wellbeing as Affective Commons

How, then, should we best pursue this idea of a more-than-human wellbeing unfolding throughout our affective environments? Neera Singh's (2017)

---

[18] See also a recent discussion by Rose, Birk, and Manning (2021) of a need to develop a "neuroecosociality" approach to mental health.

research on forest patrolling practices in Odisha, India, provides an interesting starting point. Singh described how local residents have taken it upon themselves to look after the forests and how their investment of time and care has led to a change in their attitudes. In short, a sense of affective attachment is crafted through care. Singh described this attitude as akin to "commoning," to treating the forest as a *commons*, rather than considering the environment as a resource for extraction and exploitation. These points are relevant for the discussion of wellbeing in two ways. They indicate a close connection between affective states, wellbeing, and care of others, including nonhuman others. At the same time, they point to a close link between conviviality and care and the way these attune us to others, while cultivating wellbeing, which does not simply pertain to individuals, or to the recipients of care, but to all parties involved.

My suggestion, then, is that we might consider wellbeing as a form of affective commons, to be cultivated with care, rather than seen as a good to be enjoyed individually. Just as a commons can be understood as resources used collectively and shared, an affective commons might point to shared affective resources. Unlike scarce, finite resources such as trees, however, an affective commons might be seen to thrive in circulation. For one person to feel hopeful, there need not be someone else who is left without hope. In fact, both hope and hopelessness, like so many other affects, are often contagious. The idea of an affective commons suggests a shift from a logic of scarce resources to a logic that is generative – which is to say, a logic of flow.[19]

5.4 The Logic of Flow

Care can be gifted or commoditized when embedded in particular forms of exchange. Yet, as numerous ethnographic examples in this Element show, care seems to support wellbeing most when conceived as circulating in a broader network of relations of support, rather than as a dyadic relationship between carer and cared-for. In other words, care can be conceptualized as a form of exchange between two parties but, as such, is often asymmetrical. The asymmetry becomes less of an issue when care is allowed to flow and circulate. Flow in this sense is not the state in which individuals find themselves but an enlarged circulation involving a wider range of entities and persons.

This idea can be illustrated using an example from my own research in Japan, touched on in Section 2. Networks of support and mutual aid organizations in Shimoichi rest on the idea of minimizing the burden of exchanges. Older people

---

[19] Understanding wellbeing as an affective common that circulates in environments allows us to think of it as at once subjectively experienced and cultivated with others. Thus, it is not unlike moral moods and political sentiments, discussed in Section 1.

and volunteers helped each other out, not in order that their favors to others be returned to them directly, by the very same people they cared for, or by their other neighbors. Instead, they hoped to create a general environment of support that would be there when they needed it. Rather than an exercise in reciprocity, even of a generalized kind, this is better understood as an effort to create a functioning community. While in some respects resembling a "time bank," peoples' investments of time were in this case precisely not motivated by an expectation of return. Yet while directing their actions at helping others, people contributed to the creation of a functioning community that they themselves could, in effect, also effectively rely upon. To describe these efforts in terms of self-interest would be to lose sight of the distinctiveness of the logic behind peoples' actions – what I think might better be referred to as a logic of flow.

The logic of flow does not imply calculated rational judgment, nor is it based on an underlying assumption of scarce resources. It attempts to minimize the burden of the gift, and to minimize the hierarchizing effects of giving (again in contrast to the logic of exchange). Hope does not simply spread like spilled paint, or a contagious disease; nor does it work well when understood as a scarce resource to be distributed. It is best understood as a form of the commons, flourishing in flow. Attention to the common, and to resources which, like care or love, are not diminished but rather increase with sharing, allows for quite a different conceptualization of sociality. Resources such as time, energy, or strength may be limited when construed narrowly as the properties of individuals. Yet as the abovementioned Japanese example shows us, when seen as shared they figure rather differently. Such is the logic of flow; resources in isolation dry up, in circulation they swell.

Wellbeing, similarly, is not a scarce resource or a commodity. The logic of competition in the marketplace implies that for some to come out on top, as winners, others must be left behind. When wellbeing is not seen as an attribute of individuals, however, but as a relational process – as I have argued throughout that it must – it becomes clear that wellbeing thrives in circulation. It is not an achievement nor a zero-sum game. For some to feel well, others need not feel worse. The logic of flow in which wellbeing thrives is generative. It emphasizes those resources that can flourish in circulation, such as hope (Kavedžija, 2016), care, or creativity.

If wellbeing is relational and processual, what can we attend to, beyond individual wellbeing, subjectively experienced? We can and must attend to relations of care, and to skills and practices. The flow of wellbeing, its generation in interaction, is shaped by practices modulating affect. How wellbeing moves, then, can be affected by a range of convivial arts and creative practices. Some of the convivial arts discussed in Section 1 referred to particular practices of eating and drinking together, to embodied practices such as working together (and alongside one another), but also to gauging respectful distance of a kind that facilitates engagement, and creating solitary spaces to retreat into. The time is ripe for an investigation of the full range of convivial skills in their respective contexts, alongside creative and caring practices and processes. In other words, what are the different ways in which people create the pathways along which wellbeing flows?

References

Alber, E., & Drotbohm, H. (Eds.). (2015). *Anthropological perspectives on care: Work, kinship, and the life-course*. Basingstoke, NY: Palgrave McMillan.

Alès, C. (2002). Anger as a marker of love: The ethic of conviviality among the Yanomami. In J. Overing & A. Passes (Eds.), *The anthropology of love and anger: The aesthetics of conviviality in native Amazonia* (pp. 133–151). New York: Routledge.

Anderson, S. (2015). Sociability: The art of form. *Thinking through sociality: An anthropological interrogation of key concepts*. Oxford: Berghahn Books.

Arendt, H. (1958). *The human condition*. Chicago, IL: University of Chicago Press.

Aulino, F. (2012). *Senses and sensibilities: The practice of care in everyday life in Northern Thailand*. Doctoral dissertation, Harvard University.

Aulino, F. (2019). *Rituals of care: Karmic politics in an aging Thailand*. Ithaca, NY: Cornell University Press.

Baldwin, C., Vincent, P., Anderson, J., & Rawstorne, P. (2020). Measuring well-being: Trial of the neighbourhood thriving scale for social well-being among pro-social individuals. *International Journal of Community Well-Being, 3*, 361–390.

Barber, K. (2007). *The anthropology of texts, persons and publics*. Cambridge: Cambridge University Press.

Barry, A., & Thrift, N. (2007). Gabriel Tarde: Imitation, invention and economy. *Economy and Society, 36*, 509–525.

Bateson, G., & Mead, M. (1942). Balinese character: A photographic analysis. *New York*, 17–92.

Bear, L. (2014). Doubt, conflict, mediation: The anthropology of modern time. *Journal of the Royal Anthropological Institute, 20*(S1), 3–30.

Belaunde, L. E. (2000). The convivial self and the fear of anger amongst the Airo-Pai of Amazonian Peru. In J. Overing & A. Passes (Eds.), *The anthropology of love and anger: The aesthetics of conviviality in Native Amazonia* (pp. 209–220). London: Routledge.

Bentham, J. (1983). *The collected works of Jeremy Bentham: Deontology together with a table of the springs of action and the article on utilitarianism*. Oxford: Oxford University Press.

Biehl, J. (2012). Care and disregard. In D. Fassin (Ed.), *A companion to moral anthropology* (pp. 242–263). Hoboken, NJ: Wiley-Blackwell.

Bok, D. (2010). *The politics of happiness: What government can learn from the new research on well-being*. Princeton, NJ: Princeton University Press.

Brülde, B. (2007). Happiness theories of the good life. *Journal of Happiness Studies, 8*(1), 15–49.

Buch, E. D. (2013). Senses of care: Embodying inequality and sustaining personhood in the home care of older adults in Chicago. *American Ethnologist, 40*(4), 637–650.

Buch, E. D. (2015). Anthropology of aging and care. *Annual Review of Anthropology, 44*, 277–293.

Cabanas, E., & Illouz, E. (2019). *Manufacturing happy citizens: How the science and industry of happiness control our lives*. London: Polity Press.

Candea, M., Cook, J., Trundle, C., & Yarrow, T. (2015). Introduction: Reconsidering detachment. In M. Candea, J. Cook, C. Trundle, & T. Yarrow (Eds.), *Detachments: Essays on the limits of relational thinking* (pp. 1–31). Manchester: Manchester University Press.

Chau, A. Y. (2008). *Miraculous response: Doing popular religion in contemporary China*. Stanford, CA: Stanford University Press.

Clark, S. (2009). Pleasure experienced: Well-being and the Japanese bath. In G. Mathews & C. Izquierde (Eds.), *Pursuits of happiness: Well-being in anthropological perspective* (pp. 189–210). Oxford: Berghahn Books.

Coates, J. (2017). Idleness as method. In A. Elliot, R. Norum, & N. B. Salazar (Eds.), *Methodologies of mobility: Ethnography and experiment* (pp. 109–128). New York: Berghahn Books.

Cook, J. (2015). Detachment and engagement in mindfulness-based cognitive therapy. In M. Candea, J. Cook, C. Trundle, & T. Yarrow (Eds.), *Detachment: Essays on the limits of relational thinking* (pp. 219–235). Manchester: Manchester University Press.

Corazon, S. S., Sidenius, U., Poulsen, D. V., Gramkow, M. C., & Stigsdotter, U. K. (2019). Psycho-physiological stress recovery in outdoor nature-based interventions: A systematic review of the past eight years of research. *International Journal of Environmental Research and Public Health, 16*, 1711.

Danely, J. (2015). *Aging and Loss: Mourning and maturity in contemporary Japan*. New Brunswick, NJ: Rutgers University Press.

Danely, J. (2017). Carer narratives of fatigue and endurance in Japan and England. *Subjectivity, 10*(4), 411–426.

Dasgupta, P. (1993). *An inquiry into well-being and destitution*. Oxford: Clarendon Press.

Deleuze, G. (1988). *Foucault*. Minneapolis, MN: University of Minnesota Press.

Deng, N. (2018). What is temporal ontology? *Philosophical Studies, 175,* 793–807.

Derné, S. (2016). *Sociology of well-being: Lessons from India.* Los Angeles, CA: Sage.

Dewey, J. (1980). *Art as experience.* New York: Perigee(original work published 1934).

Di Nunzio, M. (2019). *The act of living: Street life, marginality, and development in urban Ethiopia.* Ithaca, NY: Cornell University Press.

Diener, E., & Fujita, F. (1995). Resources, personal strivings, and subjective well-being: A nomothetic and idiographic approach. *Journal of Personality and Social Psychology, 68,* 926.

Diener, E., Lucas, R. E., & Scollon, C. N. (2009). Beyond the hedonic treadmill: Revising the adaptation theory of well-being. In E. Diener (Ed.), *The science of well-being. Social Indicators Research Series* (Vol. 37, pp. 103–118). Dordrecht: Springer.

Diener, E., & Suh, E. M. (2000). Measuring subjective well-being to compare the quality of life of cultures. In E. Diener & E. M. Suh (Eds.), *Culture and subjective well-being* (pp. 3–12). Cambridge, MA: MIT Press.

Diener, E., Oishi, S., & Lucas, R. E. (2003). Personality, culture, and subjective well-being: Emotional and cognitive evaluations of life. *Annual Review of Psychology, 54*(1), 403–425.

Donati, K. (2019). "Herding is his favourite thing in the world": Convivial world-making on a multispecies farm. *Journal of Rural Studies, 66,* 119–129.

Drazin, A. (2011). Towards an anthropology of care: Cleanliness and consumption in urban Romanian homes. *Slovenský národopis, 59,* 499–515.

Eloe-Fadrosh, E. A., & Rasko, D. A. (2013). The human microbiome: From symbiosis to pathogenesis. *Annual Review of Medicine, 64,* 145–163.

Enfield, N. J. (2009). Relationship thinking and human pragmatics. *Journal of Pragmatics, 41*(1), 60–78.

Farmer, P. (2004). An anthropology of structural violence. *Current Anthropology, 45,* 305–317.

Fassin, D. (2008). Humanitarianism as a politics of life. In B. J. Good, M. M. J. Fischer, S. S. Willen, & M. D. Good (Eds.), *A reader in medical anthropology: Theoretical trajectories, emergent realities* (Vol. 15, pp. 452–466). Malden, MA: Wiley.

Fassin, D. (2011). *Humanitarian reason: A moral history of the present.* Berkeley, CA: University of California Press.

Frank, A. W. (2010). *Letting stories breathe: A socio-narratology.* Chicago, IL: University of Chicago Press.

Gell, A. (1992). *The anthropology of time: Cultural constructions of temporal maps and images*. London: Routledge.

Giddens, A. (1991). *Modernity and self-identity: Self and society in the late modern age*. Stanford, CA: Stanford University Press.

Gilligan, C. (1993) [1983]. *In a different voice: Psychological theory and women's development*. Cambridge, MA: Harvard University Press.

Gilligan, C. (2011). Interview with Carol Gilligan. https://ethicsofcare.org /carol-gilligan/, accessed on April 26, 2021.

Glowczewski, B. (2019). *Indigenising anthropology with Guattari and Deleuze*. Edinburgh: Edinburgh University Press.

Gottlieb, A. (2002). New developments in the anthropology of childcare. *Anthropology News*, *43*(7), 13–13.

Gow, P. (2000). Helpless: The affective preconditions of Piro social life. In J. Overing & A. Passes (Eds.), *The anthropology of love and anger: The aesthetics of conviviality in native Amazonia* (pp. 46–63). London: Routledge.

Gowlland, G. (2019). The sociality of enskilment. *Ethnos*, *84*, 508–524.

Graeber, D. (2018). *Bullshit jobs: The rise of pointless work, and what we can do about it*. London: Penguin Books.

Hauskeller, C. (2020). Care ethics and care contexts: Contributions from feminist philosophy. *East Asian Science, Technology and Society*, *14*(1), 153–161.

Held, V. (2006). *The ethics of care: Personal, political, and global*. Oxford: Oxford University Press.

Hirsch, E., & McDonald, M. (2007). Introduction to part III: Creativity and the passage of time. In T. Ingold & E. Hallam (Eds.), *Creativity and cultural improvisation* (pp. 185–192). London: Routledge.

Hochschild, A. R. (2012). *The managed heart: Commercialization of human feeling* (3rd ed.). Berkeley, CA: University of California Press.

Illich, I. (1973). *Tools for conviviality*. New York: Harper and Row.

Inglehart, R. (2000). Globalization and postmodern values. *Washington Quarterly*, *23*, 215–228.

Ingold, T. (2013). *Making: Anthropology, archaeology, art and architecture*. London: Routledge.

Ingold, T., & Hallam, E. (2007). Creativity and cultural improvisation: An introduction. In T. Ingold & E. Hallam (Eds.), *Creativity and cultural improvisation* (pp. 1–24). London: Routledge.

Jackson, M. (2011). *Life within limits: Well-being in a world of want*. Durham, NC: Duke University Press.

Jackson, M. (2012). *Lifeworlds: Essays in existential anthropology*. Chicago, IL: University of Chicago Press.

Jackson, M. (2019). *Critique of identity thinking*. New York: Berghahn Books.

James, W. (2008). Well-being: In whose opinion, and who pays? In A. C. Jiménez (Ed.), *Well-being in anthropological balance: Remarks on proportionality as political imagination* (pp. 69–79). London: Pluto Press.

Jiménez, A. C. (2008). *Culture and well-being: Anthropological approaches to freedom and political ethics*. London: Polity.

Johnson-Hanks, J. (2002). On the limits of life stages in ethnography: Toward a theory of vital conjunctures. *American Anthropologist, 104*, 865–880.

Kavedžija, I. (2016). Introduction: Reorienting hopes. *Contemporary Japan, 28* (1), 1–11.

Kavedžija, I. (2019). "I move my hand and then I see it": Sensing and knowing with young artists in Japan. *Asian Anthropology, 18*, 222–237.

Kavedžija, I. (2020). Communities of care and zones of abandonment in "super-aged" Japan. In J. Sokolowski (Ed.), *The cultural context of aging: Worldwide perspectives* (4th ed., p. 211). Santa Barbara, CA: Praeger.

Kavedžija, I. (in press). Enskilment and the emergent imagination. In D. N. Gellner & D. P. Martinez (Eds.), *Re-creating anthropology: Sociality, matter, and the imagination* (ASA 2018 conference volume). Abingdon: Routledge.

Kavedžija, I. (in press). Loneliness as social critique: Disregard and the limits of care in Japan. In K. Barclay, E. Chalus, & D. Simonton (Eds.), *Routledge history of loneliness*. London: Routledge.

Kavedžija, I., & Walker, H. (2016). *Values of happiness: Toward an anthropology of purpose in life*. Chicago, IL: University of Chicago Press.

Keyes, C. L. M. (1998). Social well-being. *Social Psychology Quarterly, 61*, 121–140.

Killick, E. (2009). Ashéninka amity: A study of social relations in an Amazonian society. *Journal of the Royal Anthropological Institute, 15*, 701–718.

Kingfisher, C. (2021). *Collaborative happiness: Building the good life in urban cohousing communities* (Vol. 8). Oxford: Berghahn Books.

Kirksey, S. E., & Helmreich, S. (2010). The emergence of multispecies ethnography. *Cultural Anthropology, 25*, 545–576.

Kleinman, A. (2009). Caregiving: The odyssey of becoming more human. *The Lancet, 373*(9660), 292–293.

Kleinman, A., Das, V., Lock, M., & Lock, M. M. (Eds.). (1997). *Social suffering*. Berkeley, CA: University of California Press.

Kohn, E. (2013). *How forests think: Toward an anthropology beyond the human*. Berkeley, CA: University of California Press.

Kohn, E. O. (2005). Runa realism: Upper Amazonian attitudes to nature knowing. *Ethnos, 70,* 171–196.

Lambek, M. (2008). Value and virtue. *Anthropological Theory, 8*(2), 133–157.

Leonelli, S. (2021). Personal communication. Culture and Cognition group. Egenis, University of Exeter.

Lévi-Strauss, C. (1962). *Savage mind.* Chicago, IL: University of Chicago Press.

Liep, J. (2001). *Locating cultural creativity.* London: Pluto Press.

Locke, P. (2017). Elephants as persons, affective apprenticeship, and fieldwork with nonhuman informants in Nepal. *HAU: Journal of Ethnographic Theory, 7,* 353–376.

Long, N. J., & Moore, H. L. (Eds.). (2013). *Sociality: New directions* (Vol. 1). Oxford: Berghahn Books.

Marchand, T. H. (Ed.). (2017). *Craftwork as problem solving: Ethnographic studies of design and making.* London: Routledge.

Mathews, G., & Izquierdo, C. (2009). Anthropology, happiness and well-being. In G. Mathews & C. Izquierdo (Eds.), *Pursuits of happiness: Well-being in anthropological perspective* (pp. 1–19). Oxford: Berghahn Books.

McGregor, J. A. (2007). Researching human wellbeing: From concepts to methodology. In I. Gough & J. A. McGregor (Eds.), *Well-being in developing countries: From theory to research* (pp. 316–350). Cambridge: Cambridge University Press.

Mills, C. W. (1951). *White collar: The American middle classes.* New York: Oxford University Press.

Mol, A. (2008). *The logic of care: Health and the problem of patient choice.* London: Routledge.

Moroşanu, R., & Ringel, F. (2016). Time-tricking: A general introduction. *The Cambridge Journal of Anthropology, 34*(1), 17–21.

Nakamura, F. (2007). Creating or performing words? Observations on contemporary Japanese calligraphy. In E. Hallam & T. Ingold (Eds.), *Creativity and cultural improvisation* (pp. 79–98). Oxford: Berghahn Books.

Navaro-Yashin, Y. (2012). *The make-believe space: Affective geography in a postwar polity.* Durham, NC: Duke University Press.

Nikolotov, A. (2019). Volatile conviviality: Joking relations in Moscow's marginal marketplace. *Modern Asian Studies, 53,* 874–903.

Noddings, N. (2013). *Caring: A relational approach to ethics and moral education* (2nd ed.). Berkeley, CA: University of California Press.

Nowicka, M. (2020). Fantasy of conviviality: Banalities of multicultural settings and what we do (not) notice when we look at them. In O. Hemer, F. M. Povrzanović, & P. M. Ristilammi (Eds.), *Conviviality at the crossroads* (pp. 15–42). London: Palgrave Macmillan.

Nussbaum, M., & Sen, A. (Eds.). (1993). *The quality of life*. Oxford: Clarendon Press.

Nussbaum, M. C. (2013). *Political emotions*. Cambridge, MA: Harvard University Press.

O'Dwyer, S. T., Moyle, W., Zimmer-Gembeck, M., & De Leo, D. (2016). Suicidal ideation in family carers of people with dementia. *Aging & Mental Health, 20*, 222–230.

Osler, L. (2021). Bodily saturation and social disconnectedness in depression. *Phenomenology and Mind*. www.academia.edu/45613810/Bodily_saturation _and_social_disconnectedness_in_depression.

Overing, J., & Passes, A. (Eds.). (2000). *The anthropology of love and anger: The aesthetics of conviviality in native Amazonia*. London: Routledge.

Oxfeld, E. (2017). *Bitter and sweet: Food, meaning, and modernity in rural China*. Berkeley, CA: University of California Press.

Qianni, W., & Shifan, G. (2020). How one obscure word captures urban China's unhappiness. *Sixth Tone*. www.sixthtone.com/news/1006391/how-one-obscure-word-captures-urban-chinas-unhappiness.

Ratzlaff, C., Matsumoto, D., Kouznetsova, N., Raroque, J., & Ray, R. (2000). Individual psychological culture and subjective well-being. In E. Diener & E. M. Suh (Eds.), *Culture and subjective well-being* (pp. 37–59). Cambridge, MA: MIT Press.

Reinert, H. (2016). About a stone: Some notes on geologic conviviality. *Environmental Humanities, 8*(1), 95–117.

Renes, R. A., & Aarts, H. (2018). The sense of agency in health and well-being: Understanding the role of the minimal self in action-control. In D. de Ridder, M. Adriaanse, & K. Fujita (Eds.), *The routledge international handbook of self-control in health and well-being* (pp. 193–205). London: Routledge.

Ringel, F. (2016). Can time be tricked? A theoretical Introduction. *The Cambridge Journal of Anthropology, 34*, 22–31.

Robbins, J., & Rumsey, A. (2008). Introduction: Cultural and linguistic anthropology and the opacity of other minds. *Anthropological Quarterly, 81*, 407–420.

Robeyns, I., & Fibieger Byskov, M. (Winter 2020). The capability approach. In E. N. Zalta (Ed.), *The Stanford encyclopedia of philosophy*. https://plato .stanford.edu/archives/win2020/entries/capability-approach/.

Rosaldo, R., Smadar, L., & Narayan, K. (1993). Introduction: Creativity in anthropology. In S. Lavie, K. Narayan, & R. Rosaldo (Eds.), *Creativity/ anthropology* (pp. 1–8). Ithaca, NY: Cornell University Press.

Rose, N., Birk, N., & Manning, N. (January 2021). Towards neuroecosociality: Mental health in adversity. *Theory, Culture & Society*. https://doi.org/10.1177 /0263276420981614.

Sansi, R. (2014). *Art, anthropology and the gift*. London: Bloomsbury.

Sansi, R., & Strathern, M. (2016). Art and anthropology after relations. *HAU: Journal of Ethnographic Theory, 6*, 425–439.

Santos-Granero, F. (2007). Of fear and friendship: Amazonian sociality beyond kinship and affinity. *Journal of the Royal Anthropological Institute, 13*(1), 1–18.

Sapir, E. (2013) [1924]. Culture, genuine and spurious by Edward Sapir, edited and with an introduction by Alex Golub. Savage Minds Occasional Papers No. 5.

Sennett, R. (2008). *The craftsman*. New Haven, CT: Yale University Press.

Setiya, K. (2017). *Midlife: A philosophical guide*. Princeton, NJ: Princeton University Press.

Singh, N. (2017). Becoming a commoner: The commons as sites for affective socio-nature encounters and co-becomings. *Ephemera: Theory & Politics in Organization, 17*, 751–776.

Skidelsky, E., & Skidelsky, R. (2012). *How much is enough? Money and the good life*. London: Penguin.

Sneath, D., Holbraad, M., & Pedersen, M. A. (2009). Technologies of the imagination: An introduction. *Ethnos, 74*(1), 5–30.

Steinmüller, H. (2011). The moving boundaries of social heat: Gambling in rural China. *Journal of the Royal Anthropological Institute, 17*, 263–280.

Stern, L. (2020). *Diary of a Detour*. Durham, NC: Duke University Press.

Stevenson, L. (2014). *Life beside itself: Imagining care in the Canadian Arctic*. Berkeley, CA: University of California Press.

Strathern, M. (1996). Cutting the network. *Journal of the Royal Anthropological Institute, 2*, 517–535.

Suh, E. M., & Oishi, S. (2004). Cuture and subjective well-being: Introduction to the special issue. *Journal of Happiness Studies, 5*, 219–222.

Taylor, J. S. (April 30, 2014). Care: Integration. Member voices. *Fieldsights*. https://culanth.org/fieldsights/care-integration.

Taylor, J. S. (2015). On recognition, caring, and dementia. In J. Miller (Ed.), *Care in practice* (pp. 27–56). Paisley: Hodder Gibson.

Thelen, T. (2015). Care as social organization: Creating, maintaining and dissolving significant relations. *Anthropological Theory, 15*, 497–515.

Thin, N. (2008). Realising the substance of their happiness: How anthropology forgot about Homo gauius. In A. C. Jimenez (Ed.), *Culture and well-being: Anthropological approaches to freedom and political ethics* (pp. 134–155). London: Pluto Press.

Thin, N. (2012). *Social happiness: Theory into policy and practice*. Bristol: Policy Press.

Throop, C. J. (2014). Moral moods. *Ethos*, *42*(1), 65–83.

Tiberius, V. (2004). Cultural differences and philosophical accounts of well-being. *Journal of Happiness Studies*, *5*, 293–314.

Ticktin, M. (2010). Where ethics and politics meet: The violence of humanitarianism in France. In B. J. Good, M. M. J. Fischer, S. S. Willen, & M. D. Good (Eds.), *A reader in medical anthropology: Theoretical trajectories, emergent realities* (pp. 245–262). Chichester: Wiley-Blackwell.

Gough, I., & McGregor, J. A. (Eds.). (2007). *Wellbeing in developing countries: From theory to research*. Cambridge: Cambridge University Press.

Ticktin, M. I. (2011). *Casualties of care: Immigration and the politics of humanitarianism in France*. Berkeley, CA: University of California Press.

Traphagan, J. W., & Brown, L. K. (2002). Fast food and intergenerational commensality in Japan: New styles and old patterns. *Ethnology*, *41*, 119–134.

Triandis, H. C. (2000a). Culture and conflict. *International Journal of Psychology*, *35*, 145–152.

Triandis, H. C. (2000b). Cultural syndromes and subjective well-being. In E. Diener & E. M. Suh (Eds.), *Culture and subjective well-being* (pp. 13–36). Cambridge, MA: MIT Press.

Tronto, J. C. (1998). An ethic of care. *Generations: Journal of the American Society on Aging*, *22*(3), 15–20.

Tronto, J. C., & Fisher, B. (1990). Toward a feminist theory of caring. In E. Abel & M. Nelson (Eds.), *Circles of care* (pp. 36–54). Albany, NY: SUNY Press.

Tsing, A. L. (2015). *The mushroom at the end of the world: On the possibility of life in capitalist ruins*. Princeton, NJ: Princeton University Press.

Turner, V., (1970) [1967]. *The forest of symbols: Aspects of Ndembu ritual* (Vol. 101). Ithaca, NY: Cornell University Press.

Turner, V. (1977). Variations on a theme of liminality. In S. F. Moore & B. Myerhoff (Eds.), *Secular ritual* (pp. 36–52). Amsterdam: Van Gorcum.

Turner, V. (1979). Frame, flow and reflection: Ritual and drama as public liminality. *Japanese Journal of Religious Studies*, *6*, 465–499.

Tyler, K. (2017). The suburban paradox of conviviality and racism in postcolonial Britain. *Journal of Ethnic and Migration Studies*, *43*, 1890–1906.

Veenhoven, R. (2008). Sociological theories of subjective well-being. *The Science of Subjective Well-Being*, *9*, 44–61.

Vigh, H. (2009). Motion squared: A second look at the concept of social navigation. *Anthropological Theory*, *9*, 19–438.

Vigneswaran, D. (2014). Protection and conviviality: Community policing in Johannesburg. *European Journal of Cultural Studies*, *17*, 471–486.

Vilaça, A. (2002). Making kin out of others in Amazonia. *Journal of the Royal Anthropological Institute*, *8*, 347–365.

Walker, H. (2020). Equality without equivalence: An anthropology of the common. *Journal of the Royal Anthropological Institute, 26*, 146–166.

Welzel, C., & Inglehart, R. (2010). Agency, values, and well-being: A human development model. *Social Indicators Research, 97*(1), 43–63.

Wessendorf, S. (2014). "Being open, but sometimes closed." Conviviality in a super-diverse London neighbourhood. *European Journal of Cultural Studies, 17*, 392–405.

Wilf, E. (2012). Rituals of creativity: Tradition, modernity, and the "acoustic unconscious" in a US collegiate jazz music program. *American Anthropologist, 114*, 32–44.

Wilf, E. Y. (2014). *School for cool: The academic jazz program and the paradox of institutionalized creativity.* Chicago, IL: University of Chicago Press.

Wong, Y. J., Wang, S. Y., & Klann, E. M. (2018). The emperor with no clothes: A critique of collectivism and individualism. *Archives of Scientific Psychology, 6*, 251.

Yates-Doerr, E., & Carney, M. A. (2016). Demedicalizing health: The kitchen as a site of care. *Medical Anthropology, 35*, 305–321.

Zigon, J. (2018). *A war on people: Drug user politics and a new ethics of community.* Berkeley, CA: University of California Press.

Acknowledgments

This work was supported by an AHRC Leadership Fellowship (AH/T001984/1).

Cambridge Elements ☰

Psychology and Culture

Kenneth D. Keith
University of San Diego
Kenneth D. Keith is author or editor of more than 160 publications on cross-cultural psychology, quality of life, intellectual disability, and the teaching of psychology. He was the 2017 president of the Society for the Teaching of Psychology.

About the Series
Elements in Psychology and Culture features authoritative surveys and updates on key topics in cultural, cross-cultural, and indigenous psychology. Authors are internationally recognized scholars whose work is at the forefront of their subdisciplines within the realm of psychology and culture.

Cambridge Elements ≡

Psychology and Culture

.

·

Printed in the United States
by Baker & Taylor Publisher Services